RELATIONSHIP REMORSE

Mistakes Women Make When Shopping for a Man

Kathy Stafford

ePlanet Publishing, Inc.
Charlotte, North Carolina

ePlanet Publishing, Inc.
10925 David Taylor Drive, Suite 100
Charlotte, North Carolina 28262
Ph: 704-792-9092   Fax: 704-788-6694
www.eplanetpublishing.com

The information in this book is intended to be educational and entertaining. Neither the author nor the publisher guarantees that you will find love, a life partner, or make your current relationship better. Use this information at your discretion. The results are up to you. The author and publisher are in no way liable for your use or your failure to use any of the provided information.

Publisher's Cataloging-In-Publication Data
(Prepared by The Donohue Group, Inc.)

Stafford, Kathy.
    Relationship remorse : mistakes women make when shopping for a man / Kathy Stafford.

    p. ; cm.

    ISBN-13: 978-0-9793818-2-9
    ISBN-10: 0-9793818-2-7

1. Mate selection. 2. Man-woman relationships. 3. Dating (Social customs)
4. Marriage. 5. Single women--Psychology. I. Title.

HQ801 .S73 2007
646.7/7/082   2007904569

Relationship Remorse: First Printing 2007
Printed in the United States of America
Cover Design by Cara Johnston

10 9 8 7 6 5 4 3 2 1

For more information about bulk pricing for corporations, associations, and universities please contact the publisher at 1-866-200-3888, or email orders@eplanetpublishing.com.

Kathy speaks on relationship topics for both single men and women and for couples. For more information about Kathy's speaking programs visit http://www.dearkathy.com.

This book would make a great gift for someone who is struggling to find that happy relationship. To order copies of this book for family and friends, please visit Kathy's website or http://www.relationshipremorse.com.

*This book is dedicated to
single women everywhere who
still cling to the hope of finding
true love and happiness.*

Acknowledgements

I would like to thank all of my friends who have confided their hopes and dreams, sorrows and anguish, successes and regrets in their relationships. You may not have meant it when you asked for my advice, but I gave it sincerely. I hope your relationships are better for it.

In addition, I say thank you to my parents who have been married for 57 years. You have been my role models for stability and commitment in a relationship.

Thank you to the hundreds-maybe thousands now-of men and women I have worked with as a relationship coach. I think that helping professionals sometimes become too detached and clinical. Thanks for keeping me grounded by reminding me daily that your stories are real, your pain is genuine, and the hope you have for a relationship of love and commitment is universal.

I also want to acknowledge the people at ePlanet Publishing, Inc. I appreciate all their help and contributions in making this book a reality.

And, finally, thank you to my husband of 30 years, Alan. You are my inspiration, my joy, and the great love of my life.

Table of Contents

Introduction

L et's face it: most of us hate the dating process. Even if we have the skills to do it well, we still don't like to do it. We put up with dating because it is the only way-short of an arranged marriage-to meet new people and prospective mates.

This resistance to dating has several causes. First, dating strangers is actually a fairly new phenomenon. For most of mankind's existence on this planet, pairings were arranged by the two parent families. The individual man and woman had little say about whom they married. Since the marriages were pre-determined, sometimes while the couples were still young children, there was no reason to date. For millennia (that's thousands of years) dating did not exist as a social custom. Your spouse was chosen for you while you were still a child. When you reached the age considered appropriate by your family, you married the chosen partner, and that was that.

Second, within the last 100 years arranged marriages have become less frequent in our country. However, prior to World War II most people across the United States still lived on farms. If they lived in towns, the towns were small in size and few in population. Everybody knew everyone else. And since most people rarely traveled far from home, your choices for a spouse were few. And of those choices, it was almost a certainty that you knew the other person, and your parents knew his parents. In the twentieth century, you may have had a choice of marriage partners, but the choices were few and they were almost always friends of the family. Dating a stranger was rare.

With this history it is understandable that single men and women today struggle with the dating process. Who is there who can show them how to date intelligently? Who can show them the steps to take and the pitfalls to avoid? Not their parents. Both mother and father were products of a previous age-an age where you dated within your town, or your small community of acquaintances.

Today, you can meet and date someone literally on the other side of the planet. With online dating sites, instant messaging, social networking sites, cheap phone service, and relatively cheap travel, you can search far outside your geographic area and seek a mate far outside your "tribe". If you are a single adult woman today, there are approximately 40 million eligible men in the United States for you. There are about 5 million of those men within 5 years of your age. 5 Million! And 99.9999% of them are strangers.

As a single adult woman, then, the chances are high that your eventual mate will be someone your family does not know, someone you did not go to high school with, and maybe someone you haven't even met yet. Your future husband right now is a stranger. You will have to find him, evaluate him, get to know him, and test the relationship before you decide that he's the one. No group of women in history has ever had the opportunity or the responsibility to do that before. Husbands had always been known beforehand by your family and probably by you. Earlier generations of women already knew their marriage prospects. They dated, or courted, only to decide whether the acquaintance was good husband material.

No wonder people have such a hard time dating. No wonder they do it so poorly. No one has ever shown them how to do it right. That's because no one they know has known themselves. It's just not something we're taught in school. And going from "Hello" to "I do" never before involved so much work. Given these incredible changes in dating over the last 50 years, it's no surprise that marriages often don't work out. The current dating process is flawed. And by having to choose from strangers, the likelihood of a successful match goes down even more. After all, there are 5 million more men out there.

Since they're all different, how do you determine which one is best for you?

I personally believe that our distressingly high divorce rates go hand-in-hand with the social trends I've just described. We've all left the farm and moved to the big city, so to speak. But with our vastly increased number of choices in marriage partners comes an overwhelming inadequacy when it comes to weeding through them all. Selecting the good prospects and getting to know the best candidate before we marry is quite overwhelming. We are essentially flying blind in the romance area.

The results are all around us. Almost half of all marriages end in divorce. Some of these divorcees remarry once, twice or even three times but with no better results. Young people still want to be married and stay in a life-long, committed relationship, but they're scared to get married. They've seen firsthand-usually from their own parents-how sad and emotionally devastating bad marriages can be. They don't want to go through that and who can blame them.

You know what I'm talking about. Look around you. How many couples do you know who have been married 25 years or more? 30 years? 40years? As people live longer, long-term marriages should be more and more common. Instead, they are rare and are becoming rarer.

We're meeting and marrying virtual strangers. So it's no surprise that it doesn't work. We need a better way find our life's partner; to prospect in this group of strangers, screen out the bad matches, and then test the remaining candidates for compatibility. We also need a process of getting to know the other person before the wedding ceremony, even before the engagement. Marriage is not the place or time to get to know the other person. Marriage is the place to share a life together, to work toward common dreams and goals. To grow old together in love and friendship with that one special person.

Why This Book

As a married woman in her mid-forties, I have studied marriage and relationship issues with a historical perspective. I have researched the differences between the customs of my parents' generation and my own. And, I have seen the major changes in my sons' generation in the way young men and women meet, date, and choose partners. As a professional relationship coach, I have worked with hundreds-maybe thousands by now- of single men and women as well as married couples. Their experiences confirm my observations: dating in just the last ten years is unlike any other period in history. The ease of international travel and the power of the internet have made time and distance practically irrelevant when it comes to business and to dating.

My clients, and men and women everywhere, simply do not have a purposeful plan when it comes to finding their life partners. They have no family traditions, no parental wisdom to guide them. They are simply on their own in a fast-changing world that seemingly has few rules. Through no fault of their own, most of them are doing a pretty poor job of matching up and marrying successfully. And yet, they want what everyone has always wanted: a happy, fulfilling relationship of love and commitment with that one person who brings them joy and makes them feel special. Each of us wants that one companion to travel through life with. Someone to share the joys and successes of life. Someone to lean on in times of sorrow and despair. And someone to hold on to when everyone else has gone away: when the parents have passed on and the children have grown and gone. Deep down we all want that special committed relationship we call a marriage.

I wrote this book to let men and women who want to be happily married-whether they are single and looking or married and struggling-learn from the mistakes and wrong turns of others. My examples and letters from readers are not meant as putdowns or condemnations. They are, instead, stories to be learned from. Many of you will see yourselves in some of these examples. That is my intent. I want you to be able to relate to these people, to identify with them so that the people are real to you, and the learnings are real. It might have been simpler for me to just write this book as a lecture, but would you pay attention? Probably not. My message would be lost on you because it would be seen as some relationship expert trying to tell me what to do with my life. Two things I have learned as a relationship coach. One, unsolicited advice is always ignored. And two, requested advice is usually ignored.

So this is not really a book of relationship advice. It is instead a book filled with examples of what works and what doesn't when it comes to finding true love and relationship success. All the relationship mistakes in the book are taken from real people's lives and experiences. My system for finding the right person and creating your perfect relationship was developed from my extensive experience as a wife, friend, and relationship coach. You'll notice, I hope, that my system is not judgmental. My system doesn't depend on your personal values or your religious beliefs. My system is all about what works.

What You Will Get Out of This Book

Some parts of my system may rile you. You may disagree with the message and want to discredit it or otherwise discount it. That's your prerogative. But, that probably is the result of your own insecurities and state of denial. Another relationship expert, Esther Lederer, wrote a syndicated advice column under the pseudonym Ann Landers. Ann Landers had a saying that I love. Whenever a reader would write Ann a question and display an obvious sense of denial about the real problem, Ann would declare "Wake up and smell the coffee." In other words, she was telling the writer to stop denying and start acknowledging reality. A current relationship expert, Dr. Phil McGraw, uses a similar device as a reality check. He asks the aggrieved person a question, not about the situation but rather about that person's behavior in response to the situation. If you have seen him on TV, you'll know that whenever someone whines about his/her situation and his/her response to the problem, Dr. Phil simply asks "How's that working for you?" No judging, no preaching. Just a reality check: is your response to the situation getting you the results you want.

This, then, is my message as well. Heed my message or not. Follow my system, or don't. Then decide if you are getting the results you want. Is doing it your way getting you the relationship you want? If you don't like what you have, be willing and be honest enough to look at what's really going on in your relationship. And want your ideal relationship so badly that you are no longer willing to settle for something less.

When you learn from the people in this book, and when you follow my system for creating your perfect relationship, this is what you get out of this book:

- You will understand what you've been doing that keeps you from having your ideal relationship

- You will learn a simple system for expanding your choices of possible mates

- You will learn how to avoid getting stuck in bad relationships

- You will discover the real value of family connections

- You will know how to create a plan to find your perfect partner

- You will see that the long road to relationship success is actually a shortcut

Most of all, it is my sincere hope that you will learn something about yourself. If, after reading this book, you have a better understanding of your requirements and preferences in a mate, then this book will have been a success. And, if, after finishing this book, you will be able to be more honest with yourself and can search for a mate out of intention instead of neediness, then I will have done my job.

You already have the power within you to design the relationship you really want. Now, read my book and create your personal plan to go get it.

Best wishes,

Coach Kathy

Chapter One

The More Things Change . . .

For most of our existence, men have been in charge. They were the rulers of the household, the bread winners. While they went out and gathered the necessities, women were home cooking and caring for the children. This was, at first, a necessity. Men were stronger and more able to hunt and farm. But as our society became more evolved that was no longer the case. Today, women are just as capable as men in the workplace. Since most of our jobs don't require physical strength, women have a lot more choices and opportunities. They run corporations, are professional athletes and entertainers, and even go to outer space. Things have really changed for women in the past 100 years. Or have they?

Women used to be considered the weaker sex. They stayed home and cared for the children while the men did the true work. Men had the power and were the king of the castle because they earned the money. Meanwhile the women cooked and cleaned. Since women stayed home and didn't earn their own paycheck, they were dependent on their husbands to provide the home and necessities. The movement for equality between the sexes was supposed to fix all that. No longer would women be the weaker sex. Instead, women and men would have equal standing within their relationships in matters of economics, sexuality, and power. While we have made huge gains in terms of work and social standing, are we really any better off than before in our relationships?

Historically, women were the deciders when it came to sex. It was the woman who decided when to give up her virginity. It was the woman who was the pursued, sometimes by several different men. She selected the suitor who would become her mate for life. In my grandmother's day, she might have several suitors. Many men would come calling and try to win her affections. She was free to date several men at once. This was the norm. Since most of the population lived in small towns, she probably knew all the available men in her area. And the men knew all the available women. Your choice for a mate was made from within your home town. It was also not uncommon for a woman to have several offers of marriage. She would choose which man she wanted to spend her life with. Only then would she enter into an exclusive relationship and spend all her time with her one beau. Only when she had promised to marry did she limit herself to one man.

In addition to getting to know several men, women would also know their families. Since they all lived in the same town, she would know his parents and he would know hers. Part of the dating routine would be getting to know the other's family. I've heard many stories about the first time my grandfather met my grandmother's parents. I imagine it was pretty scary for him.

You might think that men would lose interest in a woman if she was also seeing other men. But it didn't happen that way. One reason she kept their interest was the exclusion of sex in the relationship. While it was common and even expected that men would have sex with 'loose girls,' those weren't the ones they married. Women had a powerful weapon in their relationship arsenal.

Today, women have given up almost all of their sexual power, and have little to show for it. There is an old saying, "why buy a cow when you can get the milk for free?" Well, today we have a glut of free milk, and a lot of cows on the market. Men know that if they start dating someone, they will probably be having sex by the second or third date. While it may be fun, it's not getting women what they want. Women are entering first marriages at older and older ages. It's not that they want to wait to get married, but it's hard to find a good man. One common complaint among these women is that most of the men they meet are either too immature or are not interested in marriage. Most of us go through a series of relationships looking for that commitment and deep love that have been fundamental keys to successful families and to fulfilling lives.

So what's going on? Women are much more willing to have sex because they think that's the way to get a man committed to them. It's not that today's women are any more promiscuous than their grandmothers were, it's just that they think that's what they need to do to get a man interested in them. After all, that's the way everyone else does it.

Men feel the pressure as well. Women expect the men they date to want to have sex early on in the relationship. One twenty-something young man told me this story. "I met Amy at a party. We talked and seemed to hit it off. I thought she was pretty and wanted to get to know her better, so I asked for her phone number. I called her a few days later and we met for a drink. I asked her out again for the following weekend. We had a great dinner and saw a movie. When I took her home, I kissed her goodnight at the door. When I called and invited her out for the next weekend, she declined. I was surprised because I thought we got along well. A few days later her best friend told me Amy didn't want to see me any more because I had not wanted to have sex with her. She thought I must be weird or something. I certainly wanted to have sex with her, but I thought it was still to early. Little did I know she was expecting me to make a move."

While this may seem like an extreme case, it's more common than you might think. I've heard women say that if the man doesn't want to have sex by the third date, he must be either really strange or gay. Why else wouldn't he want to?

The common routine today has been called serial monogamy. Despite the so-called sexual revolution and the age of free love, today's woman is not promiscuous. Contrary to what much of the popular press might have you think, most women do not sleep around. Today's women, just like today's men, enter into relationships that quickly become exclusive and are almost always monogamous. Once you start having sex with someone, you're not going to date others and have sex with them as well. The relationships continue until the almost inevitable breakdown and breakup. This relationship usually lasts from six months to a couple of years. After the break-up, the process starts all over again. The next prospective mate is chosen, the next "relationship" is entered, the mismatch is eventually realized, the breakup is concluded, and the cycle is completed, only to be followed again and again.

A number of research polls have tried to determine the values and attitudes of twenty-somethings. In almost every case, certain beliefs and values keep showing up. First, both young men and young women believe in love. Not the fiery, hormone driven type you see on TV, but rather the quieter, deeper love that takes time to grow. The kind that sustains and nurtures us throughout life. They also believe in marriage as the most enduring and desirable relationship possible. 94% of young people today describe marriage as their ideal and hope that one day they, too, will be married. And it's not just young people. More mature adults also overwhelmingly hold marriage as their ideal. Even though they may have been through a painful divorce, they still think they can find one special person to spend the rest of their life with.

The problem is most people don't know how to get that enduring, loving relationship they hope for. Our entire culture of dating, courtship, relationships, and even marriage is leading us farther and farther away from our ideal of a lifetime partnership. What we have instead is a series of temporary relationships. Dating that just leads to more dating.

One common behavior found among young singles today is called "hooking up." We used to call it casual sex. Hooking up is when you meet someone and have sex with them, knowing it will be just a one time deal. Sometimes, dates are specifically set up just to have sex. It's a planned one night stand. Sometimes, the pair will make another date to 'hook up' again. But it's always with the understanding that the point is just to have sex. There is no emotional involvement or attachment. One university study questioned why young women would agree to such behavior. The answers were surprising. A common reply was that since they are so busy with studying and other extra-curricular activities, they didn't have time for a serious relationship. So they just had a series of 'hook up' dates. After all, this was better than sitting in your room alone, wasn't it? At least it was something fun to do on a weeknight. While this may be entertaining, it's not the way to find your life's partner. And, I would submit, it's even detrimental to your search. Most women are just not able to have sex with someone and remain detached from them. Our nature is to form an emotional attachment to someone when we have sex with them. While the sexual revolution may have changed our behavior and our society's way of thinking, it could not change our physiological make-up. Most women still want to have sex with someone they like and can see on a regular basis. Yes, there are exceptions. We all know women who seem to be able to enjoy the pure physical part of sex and not become attached. But they are a slim minority.

Yet with all our newfound power and freedom, we still can't find what we're looking for. As our life expectancies expand, you would think you'd see and increase in the number of couples who've been married for 50 years or more. But look around you. How many couples do you know that have been married for 20, 30, or even 50 years? It's becoming more and more rare. In our hope of finding a life partner, we keep trying different ways.

Nobody, including the author, is arguing for a return to the days of arranged marriages. In our society, those days are gone. Women long ago were perceived as property to be sold, or given away. I can not ever see the day when women will give up their ability to choose their mate. Marriages were arranged in order to improve the financial holdings and/or social status of the family. And a woman almost always stayed true to the arrangement because she did not want to bring shame on her family. However, it is worth mentioning that when singles had fewer choices in their mates, marriages seemed to be relatively stable and tended to last until the death of one of the partners. Did we go from no choice to too many choices, or have we just not learned how to make a good choice? It does seem that we've gone much too far in the other direction when it comes to matters of the heart.

Through my experience working with hundreds of singles and couples in trouble, one thing became clear. We just don't make good choices. We either don't know how or don't take the time needed to make a good decision. Think about looking for a mate as a shopping trip. You have a party to attend and you've found the perfect dress. Now all you need is a great pair of shoes to go with it. Before you start out on your shopping trip, you think about what kind of shoes you want. Do you want high heels or flats, gold or silver, open toes or pumps? You have a good idea of what you want before you start looking to minimize your shopping time and maximize your chances of finding something suitable. Only then do you head to the mall. At the first store, you find the right style and color, but they don't have your size. Your size 9 foot just wouldn't be comfortable very long in an 8½. So you keep looking. At the next store, you find several in your size, but you wanted high heels and they only have flats. At the next store you find a pair that would do, but you're not really excited about them. Are you going to settle for that pair, or are you going to keep looking? At the fifth shoe store, you find the perfect pair.

They are just the right color, the right size, and exactly what you had in mind. So you happily take them home and are proud to wear them. It took two whole days of shopping, but you're really glad you kept looking because you really love them. You just wouldn't have been happy with the ones that were just good enough. Shouldn't you take the same care and effort when shopping for your mate? I know many of you are thinking that you've certainly put more effort into your dating than buying a pair of shoes. But the reality proves otherwise. It shows something quite different.

The divorce rate remains at over 50% of all first marriages. In our effort to better the odds, we try different methods to dating. Several troublesome trends have developed in the past decade. But there's something else in play here that adds to the instability of marriages. It's our 'me first' attitude. We have become a disposable society. We want what we want, and we want it now. When we're finished with it, we throw it away. Sadly, the same is true for our relationships. We want a serious, long-term relationship. And we want it now. So we cling to the first person who shows any promise. Maybe he's not our ideal but he fits the definition of a partner so we can have the relationship we crave. We date a few times and either throw him out or become exclusive. If we're not seeing anyone else, we must be getting closer to the relationship we want.

This leads to another disturbing trend - mini-marriages. A mini-marriage is where a couple lives together and acts as a couple, but are not truly committed to one another. They're just staying with their current partner until someone else better comes along. While there are fewer economic and social impediments to these mini-marriages, the emotional costs are enormous.

We've also seen a new phenomenon called starter marriages. Since divorce is so prevalent, many young adults just assume that their first marriage is not going to last more than a few years. So they enter into this marriage with the idea that they can end it anytime. Usually, there are no children involved so the break-up is neat and clean. Well, maybe it's financially neat and clean. But there is a huge emotional toll on people any time a marriage ends. Whether you are the one who initiates the divorce or not, it still hurts.

Most of us, however, still take marriage seriously. And most couples begin marriage with good intentions regarding the vows they spoke on their wedding day. They intend to spend the rest of their life with their spouse even though the odds are against them. So there is considerable distress and emotional trauma when that relationship ends in divorce. The current system of dating exclusively and including sex early in the relationship just isn't working. It only guarantees that we repeat the trauma and emotional pain of our past failed relationships. Living together in mini-marriages hasn't improved the odds either. And a break-up after living with someone can be just as distressful as a divorce. Maybe, just maybe, if we looked at our relationships differently we might find a way to make more intelligent choices when it comes to selecting our life partners. Maybe, we could enjoy marriages -- not relationships -- that do last a lifetime. But more than that, maybe we could find a way to make our marriages work in such a way that our lives are filled with happiness, fulfillment, and bliss.

So things have changed a lot in recent history. But are these changes for the good? Yes, we have more options, but we're not getting the kind of results we desire. I don't believe the answer is to go back to the good old days. The answer, then, lies in something else. There must be a better way, a way that will give us the end result we desire. I believe there is. By avoiding the common mistakes others have made, you can be more successful in finding a partner you can by happy with the rest of your life. Not just someone who shares the same house as you, but someone you truly love and enjoy being with. Not only will we look at the mistakes others make, but I will offer solutions for you. By following the advice in this book, you can find a lifetime of love and happiness.

Chapter Two

Mistake # 1

Shopping Without a List

We've all done it. We walk by a store window and something catches our eye. Although we weren't looking for any specific item, we saw something and just had to have it. This is impulse buying. It's what happens when you don't have a shopping list or plan. You wind up with something you really didn't need or really don't want. While its fun to impulse buy for shoes or handbags, it can lead to disaster and heartbreak in your relationships. Shopping for a partner without having a list is the first mistake women and men make.

I coach men and women every day to think with their heads, not their hormones. I advise them to be mature and systematic when it comes to searching for a mate, and to consider a number of factors beyond physical attraction when

looking for their life partner. But I also tell
them to give in to their desires. Sounds like a
contradiction, doesn't it? Let's take a closer
look.

Giving in to your desires usually conjures up
fantasies of a sexual encounter with a new flame.
You become infatuated, you move in with your
new love interest because "it just feels right", or
you agree to date exclusively because of your
own neediness and insecurity. This is not what I
mean. You give in to your desires by sticking
with your list of what you are looking for in a
mate. You allow yourself to list your
requirements, your want-to-have's, and your
nice-to-have's. In other words, you want what
you want. And it's perfectly okay.

Most of us rush into dating without any self-
analysis, without knowing what we truly want.
We never make out a shopping list. If you don't
know what you want in a mate, how will you
know when you have found him or her? Or, we
deny our wants and needs when we date. We're
so desperate to find a man (or woman) that we
settle for the first person who shows us some
attention. Then, we try to conform to the other
person's wants and needs. Women especially
"try to make it work". Arghhhh!

So give in to your desires before you begin
dating. Make a list of your dating requirements.
Be opinionated, be choosy, and be specific. It's

your life and eventually your marriage. At least start the process with your ideal mate in mind. You can always refine your list as you date more people. In fact, it's common for singles to adjust their list periodically. The only way to know what you really want is to date a number of people. As you spend time with different people and different personalities, you will be able to pinpoint those qualities you like. More importantly, you will be able to recognize the qualities you don't like. So give in to your desires. Make a shopping list for love.

Is there anything more exciting than the beginning of new a relationship? You've just met someone attractive and a courtship begins. You're filled with anticipation and desire and the possibility of impending passion. You dream about all the possibilities ahead. Maybe he's the one you've been searching for. Many times, however, we're not paying attention to our list. We wear our special rose-colored relationship glasses. So for the moment, everything is absolutely perfect. We get so swept up in the possibilities that we don't pay attention to reality.

The relationship continues for several months and finally the blinders come off. Both partners look at who they're with and discover some qualities there that they don't like. This leads to tension and stress in the relationship. As the partners try to sort through what they don't like about each other, arguments ensue. There will usually be hurt feelings from one or both sides.

Why does this take place?

The answer is simple. When we first get involved in a relationship and we're caught up in the moment, we sometimes lose sight of what it is we want. There's an initial rush of emotions flowing through us. It's called infatuation. We don't take time to really analyze the situation. We're just thinking about how wonderful it is to be in a relationship.

Let's face it, most of us have been on the same relationship merry-go-round. We meet someone who we think might be what we're looking for. They're good looking and pleasant to be with. But once we get to know them better, we find that we're not compatible with that person. We really don't have a lot in common.

What follows is the usual break-up and hurt feelings. This usually happens because we've dated for several months already and one or both partners have already developed an attachment. Once that attachment is formed, there's no easy way to end the relationship.

All of us have been there. At the beginning of the relationship, we find ourselves drawn to someone and we decide to go ahead and see where it goes. Sure, there are times when it has some real potential for a long term relationship. In those cases, it may be worth pursuing. But more often than not, your date just doesn't match your list of requirements and what you want enough for you to spend more time with them.

To give you an extreme example, it's sort of like a married couple of twenty years sitting down to dinner one night, and the husband tells the wife, "You know, honey, we just don't want the same things out of life. I think we're incompatible and I want a divorce." This has happened to more than one marriage and you've got to wonder, "You couldn't have figured this out before there were kids and a mortgage and twenty years invested in a marriage?"

So what does this mean?

Simple -- it means that you've got to know yourself.

Most of us think we know what we're all about. We're strong, independent adults who have been around a while and think we know what we like and don't like. But it's not really that simple. We've never taken the time to examine who we are, what we want, and who we want to be with the. Instead, we go through life with an image of ourselves that might not be totally accurate. We sometimes aren't even aware of things like this until we're in a relationship that isn't working and we're trying to figure out why things aren't going along as smoothly as we thought they would.

Shakespeare said, "To thine own self, be true."

On the one hand, the Bard was telling us that we have to be who we are and remain steadfast in that knowledge, but it can also be applied to our relationships. If we're not truthful about what we want in the beginning of the relationship, there's a very good chance that we're not going to have anything successful come out of it.

So your first step to successful mate shopping is to make up a list of requirements that you're going to look for in a potential mate. This is where you need to be brutally honest. Be prepared, it may not be easy. A relationship requirement is a "deal breaker". That means, if this requirement is not met, the relationship is doomed to failure. Sometimes the relationship can last for several months or even years, but sooner or later, it will end. These are basic characteristics that we must have in order to be happy in a relationship. Your list of requirements is totally up to you. It doesn't matter if your friends agree with them, or your family thinks you're crazy. After all, they aren't in the relationship. It's your relationship and your partner, so their opinion doesn't matter.

When it comes to relationships, the only opinion that matters is yours.

This is the beginning of your shopping list. When you make up your list, put down everything possible that you ABSOLUTELY MUST HAVE in that relationship. Don't hold back and don't censor yourself. No matter how stupid or silly others think it might be, put it on the list.

A friend of mine named Greg never wanted to be involved with anyone who was overweight. He met a girl, they started dating, and shortly after that, she started to put on weight. At first, Greg tried to stick it out, because he didn't want to think that he was so shallow that a girl he was once attracted to could be dumped when she put on some extra pounds. Unfortunately, no matter how hard he tried to keep that relationship on track, it turned out to be a failure.

Why? Simple -- Greg couldn't NOT be true to himself.

Needless to say, it also helps if the person you're getting involved with does the same thing. That way, both of you can start your relationship on the same page. It's better to get something out in the open at the beginning and find out that it's not going to work out, rather than wait until you're further down the line before reality sets in and you're both hurt by the experience.

Naturally, you're not going to want to go on your first date and immediately begin the interrogation. But, you should be raising some of the "list" questions after a couple of dates. That way, you can decide early on if all your requirements are there. We're talking about major issues here. Some examples may be you require that your partner be at least six feet tall; you require that your partner be of the same religion as you, you require that your partner not be physically abusive. It may be difficult to know for sure if all those requirements are there. Obviously, you may not be able to determine in the first few weeks of dating that your partner will be faithful. But you can talk about past relationships and see if that behavior has been there in the past. If you don't like the picture that's forming, you can end it quickly and before it goes too deep.

There's another reason why it's a good idea to know what's a deal breaker from the very beginning.

When a deal is broken, you can walk away without feeling bad -- because you set up the ground rules at the beginning of the relationship.

For example, let's say one of you're requirements is that your partner never cheats on you. First of all, that needs to be made clear at the beginning of the relationship. This way, your partner will understand that this is very important to you. If they are tempted later on down the road, they might think twice. They know that if they break this deal, you're going to be out of that relationship.

And here's where you have to be true to yourself. If you have something that is a deal breaker and your partner breaks that deal, you need to end it right then and there. Do not fall into the trap of going back on something that is important to you. Otherwise, you're going to wind up compromising yourself more and more. You may prolong the relationship, but you will not be happy. Eventually, the relationship will fail and you'll be scolding yourself for sticking with it for so long.

One word of caution, this list will likely be very short. Since this is your list of absolutes for your relationship, make sure you only put things here that you definitely have to have. Keep in mind that if these requirements are not met, you will end the relationship.

So now you have a basic shopping list. You've successfully come up with a list of deal breakers. Terrific! It's time to start working on another list.

This list is going to be "wants." These are items that are not absolute requirements, of course, but they're going to help you find out what areas of the relationship are going to work out the best for you. For example, you might decide that you want someone who loves dogs since you have two lap dogs. This isn't a deal breaker. You can have a great relationship with someone even if he isn't crazy about animals. But you will find the relationship is easier if your partner is a dog lover as well. Someone else could have a dog-lover on their list of requirements. This is a personal choice.

Dear Kathy,

I am in a relationship with a man I'll call John. We've been dating for 2 years and have been living together for the past year. When I met John, I knew he was a smoker. I really detest the smell of smoking, but he was so good looking and we got along so well. He promised that he'd quit smoking since I dislike it so much. Here we are 2 years later and he still smokes. We argue about this all the time and it's ruining our relationship. What should I do?

Mary

Dear Mary,

You've made the same mistake many women make. You may not realize it, but a non-smoker is on your list of relationship requirements. You knew this but thought you could get John to quit and things would work out okay. Since he obviously doesn't intend to stop smoking, your only choice is to end the relationship. You can already see that yourself, you just needed someone to tell you. As long as he still smokes, this relationship is doomed. It's time to move on and find someone who is more compatible, and who doesn't smoke.

Mary made the mistake of not being true to her desires. A non-smoker was on her list of requirements, but she didn't stick with it. Because John was so handsome and she wanted to make the relationship work, she tried to ignore her list. Now she finds that she's spent two years with him and the relationship is ending. No matter how hard she tries, she still doesn't like to be around smokers. If she had been true to herself in the beginning, this relationship would never have started. She would have refused to date him once she discovered his smoking. She wouldn't have wasted the past two years in a relationship with someone who could never be her life's partner.

And she would have spared them both the hurt feelings that will come from the break-up.

If smoking had been one of Mary's wants rather than a requirement, the relationship might have worked. Mary would be annoyed by John's smoking, but she may have been able to put up with it if John agreed to smoke only outside and not in the apartment. If all of her requirements were being met and most of her wants, Mary may decide that the smoking is not a deal breaker. This is the difference between requirements and wants.

And, lastly, there are the "nice to have" items. These are things that aren't a requirement and aren't of paramount importance but they might just add a little something extra to the relationship. These are the things that you can live without in your relationship but they sure would make the relationship even more satisfying.

Let's relate is back to our shopping. We're looking for some new shoes. They must be high heels in our size (requirement). Our dress is black so we'd like to have silver shoes, but black would also work (want silver, but not a requirement). We'd also like to have open toes and pay less than $75 (a nice to have item).

These items are different from person to person. One person might have "must love foreign films" as an absolute requirement, while another person has that on their "nice to have" list. Neither person is right or wrong in a situation like this. That's why it's important to take some time in the beginning to make your list. Understand that you need to sit down by yourself and decide what is important to you.

Some of you might be thinking that this whole "list" regimen is kind of silly. After all, you know what you like. You don't have to write it down. Perhaps you've been in the dating game for several years. You surely know by now what type of people you like or don't like. But unless you make a list, you can never be really clear. Making a list will force you to clarify to yourself your requirements, wants, and niceties. Your list is not set in stone, however. You can continually add to it. Some people find that an item they once considered a mere want is really a requirement for them. The only way to be sure is to write it down. If you're not sure what you're looking for in a potential partner, how are you going to actually meet them? You need to have a clear understanding of what you want before you can ever hope to find it

Are you beginning to understand why over ninety percent of all relationships fail? This is what happens when the parties involved don't understand what it is that they're looking for. Not only will the right person be harder to find, you may not even recognize them when you see them. Having a list makes it easier to spot potential partners when you meet them.

If you're not aware of what you're looking for, you leave finding the right relationship to mere chance. It doesn't have to be that way. You have more control over the process than you realize.

You can succeed. You can find the right partner for you. However, in order to succeed, I'm going to ask you to do something that you might not have thought about doing before.

I'm going to ask you to rethink your entire dating strategy.

As we've talked about, the first thing I want you to do is sit down and write your list of requirements. Do this alone and without any input from anyone else. Don't ask your friends what you should put on the list. Don't ask for your mother's advice. Don't even check with your sister to find out what she thinks about the process.

You're the only one involved with this stage of the game because you're the only one who can determine precisely what you want.

If you think that it's going to be easy to come up with this list, think again. Believe it or not, most of us go through our lives without fully knowing who we are and what we want. This isn't a criticism, by the way. It's just the way we happen to be. We were never taught to think about relationships this way. No one ever told us we needed at shopping list or a dating strategy.

So we go through life on "auto pilot." Oh, we have a general idea of what we're looking for and we think we're going to know it when it comes along. But that's not necessarily the case. If we don't know what our requirements are, we're never going to know when we meet someone who might have met them. More importantly, we won't recognize when someone isn't worth our time in the first place.

Okay, let's take a look at how you're going to find out what your requirements are. The good news is that it's not that hard. It may take some time, but it shouldn't be that taxing. Since requirements are very basic items, this list probably won't be very long. The bad news is you may have to rethink another part of your dating strategy.

To find out what your requirements for a perfect partner are, you have to do a lot of dating. Only by dating a lot of different people will you begin to notice what qualities you like and don't like.

At this point, it's important to note that I didn't say you have to have sex with a lot of people.

After all, you can have a lot of sex and not really get to know anyone. By the same token, I'm not suggesting that you dive right into an exclusive long-term relationship. You could waste a lot of time only to decide this is not heading in the right direction for you.

You see, part of what's wrong with the approach most people have to dating is that they are "serial daters."

Here's the typical scenario: you to meet someone, go out on a few dates, have sex with that person, get exclusive, develop emotional attachments, have a fight, break up, and begin the process all over again.

Using this strategy, you will date between 3 to 8 people before you reach the stage in your life where you want to get really serious about someone and move on to the engaged/married stage. That's not the way to do it.

The key to success in finding the right person for you is to "parallel date." Parallel dating means that you date 2, 3 or 5 people at the same time. (At this point, I need to explain that we're talking about dating "at the same time" and not "on the same day." We want you to find the perfect partner -- not wind up in some kind of French romantic comedy farce.)

Here are some statistics to consider when you think about the benefits of parallel dating and of finding your soul mate:

- 1/2 of all first marriages end in divorce.
- 2/3 of all second marriages end in divorce.
- 3/4 of all third marriages end in divorce.

You can see why it's important that you find the right person, and in order to do that, you will have to go through a lot of people. And since second and third marriages don't fare any better than first marriages, the current trend in relationships is obviously not working for most of us.

You should realize that dating is not a "relationship." Dating is just dating. It's where you get to know the other person and find out whether or not the two of you may right for each other.

When you parallel date, you'll find that some of the people you meet will be eliminated after one or two dates. You'll get a sense that they're not what you're looking for, and you'll move on. It's quick and easy. You might date other potential partners three or four times before you decide they're not right for you.

When you've dated twenty or thirty or fifty people, it will become very clear to you what you like and what you don't like in a potential partner. While this is especially true of younger adults, it applies to people of all ages. And it applies equally to men and women. Most of us don't do a lot of comparison shopping in our relationships. If that's the case, how are you going to know what to look for? Sure, there are always exceptions. You probably know people who dated in high school, got married young, and remained married for 50 years. But they are the exception, not the rule.

The reason Parallel Dating works is because it doesn't rely on deep introspection and navel-gazing. Your list is derived from actual dating experience and not some fantasy notion of what we think our partner should be like. Besides, many of us can trick ourselves into thinking that we want something in a partner that we really don't want. My friend, Frank, was sure he knew what he was looking for in his future wife. He wanted someone who was very nurturing and motherly toward him. However, the person who turned out to be his perfect mate actually is very independent and is as far from being motherly to him as you could ever imagine. When I asked him why he had been looking for the motherly type, he admitted that it was because he "thought" that's what he wanted. He had a fantasy of someone who would be just like his mother. But the reality was that he didn't like being treated that way by anyone else but his mother. It took him a long time to figure this out. Had he been out there parallel dating, he would have seen more quickly that one of the elements all of his enjoyable relationships had was that the potential partners were independent.

Another friend of mine, Lydia, always went out of her way to date "sensitive" men. None of those relationships ever lasted, though, and when she sat down and really examined what she was looking for in a man, she realized that she actually wanted a strong and "take charge" kind of partner. Once again, had she parallel dated, she would have determined this more quickly and not wasted so much time on the sensitive men who did not suit her.

So, you're on the road to parallel dating but you're not sure what to do. First of all, don't pass up a date with a potential partner just because you've been out with someone else. Remember, this is the whole premise of parallel dating. You can, and should, date more than one person at a time. When you find that someone isn't making the grade, stop seeing them. This could be in a few as one or two dates. Or it could be one or two months. It's up to you. When one person is taken off the list, it frees up time for someone else to come into the picture. This is the opposite of "settling."

My mother would always say, "Cereal settles. People shouldn't."

What you're doing is surveying the field, deciding what your requirements are, and then dating and being selective until you find the people out there who meet your requirements.

When you're working on your lists, be brutally honest with yourself about each requirement. Examine each one and ask yourself, "Is this truly something that would have me walking out the door if it was broken?"

You might be surprised at how few "deal breakers" there are. For example, many people assume that infidelity is a deal breaker. But, what if you were married to someone for twenty years, you had great children, a good home, and a marriage that is, for the most part, happy and loving? But, you find out that your partner had a one-nighter last year. It was a one-time thing, your partner is desperately sorry, and it's over. Now you have to decide if you're going to throw away twenty good years because of it. You may not end your marriage of twenty years because of one night of infidelity. But do you want to stick with a new relationship with someone who if unfaithful?

The other lists are your "want" and "nice to have" lists. These are going to be longer than your deal breaker list, and they're just going to be there to guide you when you're going through the entire dating process. These lists will be your recruiting tools when it comes to deciding whether or not you even want to pursue a relationship with someone.

I know that some of you out there might be finding the whole idea of looking for your potential partner in such a calculated manner to be very unromantic. Well, breakups and divorce are not romantic, are they? But when it comes to certain misconceptions, and lasting relationships are one of them, studies have shown that romance doesn't necessarily mean "long-lasting." Romance always fades. The relationships that last are those that are built on mutual understanding and compatibility.

When you go out on your next date, think about your list. As your date progresses, you're either going to eliminate that person from future dates (if it turns out they aren't meeting the requirements on your list) or you're going to go out on a second date with them. On the next date, you will learn more about them to find out whether or not the two of you should continue dating.

By the end of the second or third date, you should be able to determine whether or not most of the requirements on your list are being met. At that point, you can continue dating or decide not to date them any more. With each date your will learn more and more about them. Any time you find that your requirements will not be met, you can discontinue dating them. The more you date, the easier it will be to determine if that person is suitable for you. The point comes when either the person you're with is eliminated from the dating pool, or you move the relationship to the next stage.

By following this advice, you will have "pre-eliminated" a lot of partners who just couldn't make the grade. And you'll maximize your chances for finding a suitable partner. By the time you decide you're going to spend the rest of your life with this partner, you'll have maximized your chances for a successful marriage. Parallel dating can maximize your results and you can be one of the successful ten percent of all relationships.

Don't make the same mistake that most people make when dating. Take time before your next date to write out your list of requirements, wants, and "nice to haves". Remember, there's nothing wrong with dating smartly and efficiently. By avoiding the common mistake of not knowing what you want to begin with, you have a better chance of finding your perfect partner. So know what you want before you go out there and try to find it.

Chapter Three

Mistake #2

Needing to Be in a Relationship

Relationships are an extremely important part of our lives. When we look around, we find that there are relationships we have between ourselves and our families, ourselves and our friends, ourselves and our co-workers. It's been said that no man is an island, and for the most part, that's true. With very few exceptions, most of us need and want relationships in our lives. Not just one or two, but a lot of them. It's what makes life interesting.

When it comes to romantic relationships, we have to understand that these are good and natural. It's our very nature to pair off – and it's only natural for society to recognize and honor those who do so. But while we feel good when we are involved in a romantic relationship, there's another side as well.

Many people feel worthless when they are not in a relationship. They sit at home, alone and unattached, and they find themselves with feelings of low self-esteem and loneliness. These people are the ones who seem to think that they're only worthwhile when they are part of a couple.

I'm sure you've known people like this — the ones who are out there, constantly in a relationship. The minute that one relationship ends (and trust me, it's going to end), they jump right in to a new relationship. If they're in between relationships, they are in a kind of "panic mode," not knowing what to do with themselves, not knowing what they have to do in order to change so that they can be in a relationship.

My friend Karen is a perfect example of this. When she's in a relationship, she's on Cloud Nine. Everything's right with the world, nothing can go wrong, there are going to be no raindrops falling on her parade. But, when the relationship goes south — as it always does — she launches herself immediately into a new relationship. Before she can even digest what went wrong with the relationship that she was in, she's out there, looking for another man to get involved with. Another man to make her happy.

For too many people, they rely on that relationship to give them purpose. I'll be the first one to admit that it's worthwhile and rewarding to be in a good relationship, but having a partner does not complete you.

You are already complete.

There are so many people out there who don't understand this basic concept. As far as they're concerned, the only way they're going to be complete is when there's someone else in the equation. The old myth about finding your soulmate started that way. It was said that man started out with two heads. When one was cut off, he was destined to search his whole life until he found that one special head that would again make him whole. Each person had only one that would make him complete again and he kept looking until he found it. Only then would his life be complete. But, remember, it's only a myth.

I want you to understand something – finding your soulmate does not mean you're going to find someone to complete you. Rather, it means you're going to find someone to complement you. There is an important distinction between the two. Someone who complements you is someone who helps you be a better person. They bring out the good in you and minimize the not so good. They highlight your great qualities and downplay your faults. And we all have faults. Just don't expect someone else to make you whole. You can not depend solely on another person to make you complete.

Does this mean I'm telling you that you shouldn't want to have a relationship? Of course it doesn't. What I'm telling you is that you shouldn't NEED to be in a relationship.

If you're someone who thinks you always need to be in a relationship, you are going to go out there and search until you find someone to have a relationship with. It doesn't matter much who they are. You just want someone, anyone, to be your partner. You'll do it without thinking, without close examination, without consideration because the goal is to be in a relationship. And you'll do it for the worst possible reason — because you're desperate.

What happens when someone is desperate? First of all, they begin to do things that they normally wouldn't do. If you watch basketball, you'll see a good example of this behavior in many games. The clock is winding down to 3 seconds, 2 seconds. Suddenly, someone throws up a 3 point shot. They would never, under normal circumstances, take a shot from that far away, but they're desperate because time is running out. We do the same thing in our relationships. We get desperate and start thinking time is running out. Then we do things we normally wouldn't do. Sure, it's easy to stick to your guns when everything is going smoothly, but what happens when things get bumpy? We usually see one of two things. You can either slow down and move more carefully, or you can swerve and ride on the side of the road.

In other words, once you've taken the time to make your list of requirements you have to stick with them. If, all of a sudden, things don't seem to be going the way you want, you might be tempted to put your list to the side and get into a relationship anyway.

Don't do it. If you're sincere about finding the person who will be right for you, this means that you've got to be strong in your determination and you've got to understand that it's going to take some time. Don't just jump into a relationship because your clock is ticking – and I'm not talking about your biological clock, either.

I'm talking about your relationship clock.

Whenever we end a relationship, our clock begins to tick. At first, we don't pay much attention to it, because we're just getting over the relationship that went wrong. Maybe we still have feelings of hurt and anger and we don't want to think about relationships too much. It does take some time to get over a failed relationship whether we are the one who chose to end it or not.   But, sooner or later, we become aware of the clock, and we start to think,

"Gee, I haven't been in a relationship for a long time.   I really don't like being home alone and it would be nice to have someone to do things with.   Besides, I'm really not very good on my own.   I'd better think about getting another relationship before I wind up dying alone and unloved."

For some people, this thought comes months after a relationship has ended.   For others, it appears within minutes, it seems.   In order for you to find the person who is going to be the right one for you, you have to throw that darn clock out the window.

It's what gives you the feelings of desperation — and that means that you'll probably make some poor choices.

Dear Kathy,

I'm a divorced woman in my 40's. I've just ended another relationship and I don't know what to do.   I saw this man exclusively for over 5 years.   He even proposed to me and we were engaged for a time.   I really want to get married again, but I finally realized that I just couldn't marry him.   The more time I spent with him, the more I realized he didn't make me happy. We really had nothing in common. I like to do things outdoors, and he did not. I like going out to eat and shop, and he was a home body. I guess I kept hoping he would change but he never did. Now I'm five years older and starting all over again. Why do I keep getting stuck with the wrong men?

Shelly

Dear Shelly,

You keep getting stuck with the wrong men because you aren't willing to wait for the right one. If you have a dating plan and a list of requirements, you should be able to tell after a few dates whether someone could possibly be right for you. Don't stick with someone just because you so desperately want a relationship. Had you determined earlier on in your relationship that he was not right for you, you wouldn't have spent 5 precious years with the wrong man only to have it still end. My advice is that you make a list of your relationship requirements and 'want to haves'. The next time you start dating someone, compare them to your list. If they don't meet all of your requirements, move on to the next one. Better to do so early on than to spend so much time on the wrong one.

Shelly is a good example of what happens when we need to be in a relationship. She got involved with someone who was not right for her and almost married him because she wanted so badly to have a relationship. Even though she was not happy, she kept hoping things would get better. She just took herself off the dating market for five years while she tried to make it work. Many of us have made the same mistake. But I want you to learn from Shelly. So take your time before you jump into a relationship with someone, anyone, just so you're not alone.

If you find yourself afraid of being alone, you're very likely to settle for someone who isn't right for you. You'll latch onto someone, and get involved with them before you completely think things through.

The next thing that happens in the relationship is that you realize the two of you aren't a good match. It might take you some time to reach this point. Much of that depends on if you adhere to your relationship list. Usually, people who fall quickly into the next relationship don't even have a list. They don't spend any time thinking about what they want because they just want a relationship. So there will come a point when you wake up to reality, look at the relationship, and decide that the two of you are not what you thought you were. But you really want this to work. Not because you really love the person, but because you don't want to be alone again.

What happens, then? Well, if you're like millions of other people who have had "relationship remorse," you'll try to make the relationship work. You dislike the idea of being alone. And how are you going to go about doing that? The first reaction is the simplest one.

You're going to try to change the person that you're involved with. All of a sudden, you're getting thoughts in your head that go along the lines of:

"If only he made more money..."

"If only she didn't spend so much time with her girlfriends..."

"If only he wasn't such a slob..."

"If only she wasn't such a neat freak..."

"If only he didn't watch so much football..."

"If only she was into football..."

You get the idea. It's not as if you have to change yourself to make the relationship better. After all, you're fine just the way you are. Your partner needs to do the changing. Although studies have shown that most people don't change much once they reach adulthood (around the early twenties), you think he'll change if you just work on him some.

This is when the turbulence in a relationship starts.

For many of us, when we think about something we want to change in the other person, it usually involves having that person stop some behavior that's been part of them for a long time. If you're a woman, it might involve having your partner stop watching sports all the time, or not drinking so much beer. If you're a man, it might be something along the lines of wishing that your partner wouldn't go shopping with her girlfriends so often, or stop changing the radio channel in your car. Many times, it's something that's part of their behavior pattern you've seen since you started dating. So even when you first entered the relationship, you knew these things were going on.

You might have even recognized from the beginning this behavior. You thought you were going in with you eyes wide open, but you're also thinking, "I don't like the way he does this" or "I hate the way she does that." And you were also thinking, "Once we're together, though, I'll get them to stop doing that. Once he loves me, he'll stop if I ask him to." You may have also thought that it really wasn't a big deal. You'd just be able to ignore that part of his behavior or put up with it. Remember, this is why we make a relationship list. So we don't have to try to put up with things that annoy us.

However, there's a flip side to this, as well. There are people who want their relationships to work so badly that they'll try to change themselves. They pretend to be someone other than who they are, just to keep the relationship going. I'm sure you've known someone like that. You probably have friends who are like that. You might even be someone like that.

I'm here to tell you, right now, that it's not going to work.

I don't care who you are and I don't care how hard you pretend, you are not going to make that relationship work. Oh, you might get away with it for a little while, you may even get away with it for a long while, but there will come a point when you're just going to get fed up with not being able to be who you are. Finally, you're going to have to drop the pretense.

My friend Janine went through that very thing. She met a guy named Tony, and they hit it off. However, she knew that Tony liked women who were into foreign movies and intellectual pursuits. Janine had always found things like that pretentious and boring, but because she wanted to be in this relationship, she went along with it.

"It was torture," she said, telling me about the relationship. "I'd sit with Tony and we'd be watching a movie that I couldn't understand anything about. It was like the director was on a bad drug trip. Then, when the movie was over, we'd go out to some coffee house somewhere and I'd have to listen to Tony explain what the movie meant and why it was such a great film. I still didn't see the point. It was even worse when we got together with his friends, because they were even more pretentious than he was. But, I stuck with him, because I thought that I could eventually learn to like the things that he liked. I thought if I just watched a few more of those movies I'd learn to understand and appreciate them the way Tony did. It lasted for about six months. But one night, we were in an art house and he was standing in front of this painting that literally looked like someone's cat had hacked up hairballs on it. Tony explained to me that the artist was trying to make a statement about the oppression of government in the lives of the individual and I just couldn't take it any longer – I burst out laughing. I said, "Where do you dream up this stuff?" He got offended, but I couldn't help myself. I suddenly saw how foolish and ridiculous he looked. What's more, I realized that I was trying to get to be more like him, and that made me laugh even harder. Needless to say, the relationship ended after that."

Knowing yourself and who you are is so important in any relationship, and in life, as well. Great relationships come from two people who know who they are and know each other. People like that generally seek out compatible souls to journey with, and that's why you need to know who you are.

To use a shopping example, sometimes, being in a relationship is like needing a new pair of shoes for a party. It's an important party, and you have to be there. The thought of missing out on this party is stomach-churning. Time is running out, though, and you need to get a pair of shoes for the party tonight. You race across town, and you find a shoe store that has a shoe that's almost the right style and almost the right color. Unfortunately, it's a half-size too small.

But, you really, really want to be at that party, so you get the shoes anyway. You put them on and off you go.

Now, when you're at the party, when you should be enjoying yourself, what are you doing? You're standing there, your feet in agony, hating every minute that you're there. At this moment, you are experiencing the dreaded "buyer's remorse," and you can't believe you were ever stupid enough to buy these shoes. What were you thinking?

As soon as you get home, you throw off those shoes, toss them into the back of the closet, and you never wear them again. Why? Because settling for the wrong pair of shoes does not work.

Why in the world would you think that settling for the wrong man in a relationship would?

Part of the problem comes from this society. If you go to just about any high school, you'll find that many of the girls HAVE to have boyfriends. Period. These girls think that they're defined by who their boyfriend is and what his status in the school is. Of course, you're thinking, they're just silly teenagers. But remember that people don't really change their personalities that much as they get older. There are plenty of adult women – and men – who think exactly the same way.

I know men who can't be outside of a relationship. They think that something's wrong with them if they don't have a woman in their life. And, I know many women who think the same thing about men. If they are not in a relationship, they consider themselves failures and they usually wind up going through a period of great depression.

Some of the blame for this can be laid at the feet of society. Women were told stories from a young age about the awful fate awaiting some. We all know the stereotype of the spinster – as if being single was the worst fate that could befall a woman. Think back to the fairy tales you heard as a child. Everyone ended up living happily ever after, and they all had a handsome prince by their side. There are no fairy tales where the woman lives happily ever after being alone.

Another problem with needing to be in a relationship is that when we place paramount importance upon the relationship itself, we tend to be a little "flexible" in our choice of partners. This leads us to sometimes waking up and finding ourselves in bad relationships and staying in them because we feel that being in a bad relationship is better than not being in a relationship at all.

Wrong.

Yes, I think that men and women have a need to be committed to each other – be it to support each other emotionally, parentally (if there are children involved), spiritually, or even, physically. We're all on this great journey that we call Life, and we want to have someone traveling with us.

That's what being in a good relationship is all about. But, if you find yourself in a bad relationship, there is no need to stay in it. You see, being single is light-years better than being in a bad relationship.

From best case to worst case, here is the order of value in a relationship:

Good marriage (best)
Being single (good)
Bad marriage (not good)
Bad relationship (worst)

So, what this means is that it's okay to want a relationship, as long as you're willing to avoid the bad relationships and wait for the good ones. If you realize that being single is better than being in a rotten relationship, you'll have the patience to wait till someone compatible comes along. Remember this – there may be times in your life when you have no good choices.

That's fine.

Stay single, and enjoy it.

Congratulate yourself that you've chosen to remain single and that you've had the good sense not to get into a relationship that would be bad for you, just so that you can say you're in a relationship.

Two women meet for coffee. The first woman says, "Did you hear about Ellen? She's got a boyfriend who cheats on her, steals from her, and wrecked her car!" The second woman responds with, "How come Ellen can find a boyfriend and I can't?"

I'm not considered a feminist, but there are certain areas where I find myself in agreement with them. One of them is when it comes to the value of self-worth. Whoever you are and whatever it is that you do in life, it's important to understand that you are valuable on your own. You do not need to have a partner to have value in our society.

Yes, it's okay to want to have a partner so that you can share a couples' relationship that is impossible by yourself. However, you are complete, even without that relationship. You should never have to depend on someone else to 'complete' you.

It's better to be single and wait to find the right relationship, rather than to be part of a couple in a bad relationship.

Now, some of you might be wondering what you can do if you decide to wait for the right relationship. After all, if you're single, you're going to have some spare time on your hands. And you just don't like sitting home alone or going out to dinner alone. It's okay to not like doing things alone. Get a girlfriend to meet you for dinner. Join a book club or bowling league. Find something that interests you and you can almost always find a group of people who have the same interests. Work on who you are and refining what it is that you're looking for.

Life is a series of decisions. When we wake up in the morning, we decide whether or not we're going to jump right out of bed, or if we're going to sleep in for a few more minutes. When we get ready for work, we make a decision as to what clothes we're going to wear. Are we going to pack a lunch to take with us, or are we going to go out for lunch today?

This means that you can also make the decision as to whether you're going to be happy or not, and whether you're going to like yourself as you are or not. Part of working on your self is taking time to really examine yourself. You may find some things you don't like. If you're constantly late for meetings but don't like that behavior in others, work on being more prompt. The next time you agree to meet your girlfriends for dinner, make sure you get ready in plenty of time so you can arrive on time. You may even want to arrive 5 minutes early. If you don't like that behavior in others, they probably don't like it in you either. You can work on little things like that while you're searching and waiting for someone you like to come along.

So, you're going to wait for that perfect partner, but that doesn't mean that you're just sitting on the couch, looking at the phone, waiting for it to ring.

Work on ways that you can create your own satisfying, rewarding life as an individual. You can do such diverse things as further your education, or build deeper friendships, or look into new hobbies. It's your life to do with as you will. And you can make it a grand life as a single person.

Once you decide that you're okay on your own, something else usually happens. The more rich and fulfilling you make your life as a single person, the more likely it is that you're also going to find yourself meeting more people who might well meet your requirements for a partner.

Dear Kathy,

It was when I went back to college after my divorce that I took a psychology class. We got on to the subject of finding out who you are. I was single again and was having a hard time dealing with it. I decided that I finally wanted to figure out who I was. So I started to do things that I had always wanted to do. Things I had never done because I was always having relationship problems. One of the things that I did was take an art class. I'd always wanted to learn how to paint, but I just didn't seem to have the time. It was in my art class that I met Eric, who turned out to be the man that I married. Looking back on it, I have to admit that if I hadn't been on my own, and if I hadn't chosen to branch out into new directions, I probably never would have met him. I'm so glad I took your advice and learned to be okay on my own. Had I jumped right into another relationship, I never would have met the man of my dreams.

Caroline

The lesson you need to learn from Caroline is to live your life to the fullest each day. Don't keep on chasing those "someday," as in "Someday, I'll do this..." or "Someday, I'll do that..."

If you need a relationship to make yourself feel happy or complete, you're asking too much from the relationship. Sure, at first, you might think that all of your needs are being met, but you'll discover that you need more...and more...and more...

Eventually, you'll realize that nothing in the relationship is going to make you happy if you're not happy with yourself. You'll end up being disappointed and disillusioned again. If you're not happy with who you are, you can not expect someone else to be able to make you happy. I have a dear friend who suddenly announced that she was leaving her husband after 20 years of marriage. It's not that he did anything wrong or had changed in any way, she just wasn't happy. She thought she wanted time to do things on her own, to make her own decisions, to live her life the way she'd always wanted. After being on her own for a couple of years, she finally realized that the problem was her. It wasn't that her ex-husband didn't make her happy; it's that SHE didn't make her happy. And nobody else could fix that but her. She's happy being herself now, but it's too bad she had to throw away a 20 year marriage to find this out.

So work on who you are first, and who you want to be.

Here's the real secret. Something amazing happens when you're comfortable with being who you are, and when you're comfortable with being single. That comfort is going to come across as confidence, and that is a huge turn-on for people. We've all met needy people, and we all know what turn-offs they are. In fact, when most of us see a needy person, we tend to head in the opposite direction – at a very fast pace. We have enough going on in our lives without having someone else constantly relying on us for their own satisfaction.

Many of my clients have told me that once they've gotten to a comfortable place in their lives with who they are, that's when someone great comes along. There's a reason for this. If you're looking for someone terrific, chances are that they're looking for someone terrific as well. They're going to want to meet someone who is confident being by themselves, someone who doesn't need a relationship. Remember – you need to love and accept yourself before you expect anyone else to do the same.

Don't make this common mistake. In healthy relationships, couples are together because they want to be together – not because they need to be together. When you have two people who are comfortable with themselves in a relationship, you'll discover the relationship is usually based on mutual love and respect.

Chapter Four

Mistake #3

Having Sex Too Soon

I magine you are at your favorite mall. On your way to the shoe store, you walk by a pet store. In the window are the cutest, fluffiest puppies you've ever seen. You are drawn to them and start to think about how much fun it would be to have one of your own. You go inside where you can hold and play with them. Before you know it, you're on your way home with you adorable new friend. It's really cute and fun − for about a week. Then it starts to chew on your shoes, shred the newspapers you put down for it, and whine at night when you're trying to sleep. And forget about going off for the weekend, you can't leave it alone for a few days. Reality sets in and you realize you've made a mistake getting the puppy. You were so blinded by how cute it was that you didn't stop to think about what it would really be like to own one.

Entering a sexual relationship with someone can be like that puppy in the window. You meet someone who's really cute. You're drawn to them. You start dating and before you know it, you're having sex.

We all know that sex is an important part of just about every relationship. It can bring us to a new level of closeness with our partner. For many people, it is extremely vital to maintaining a healthy partnership.

Naturally, though, there is a time and a place for sex.

When we were growing up, we were told that most people saved themselves for marriage. Well, that wasn't quite the truth. The idea that most women are going to be virgins on their wedding days is a nice fairy tale to tell the children, but it's probably never been close to the truth. Even in previous generations, the number of virgin brides was exaggerated.

Study after study has shown that most men are not virgins by the time they are twenty-one. And more than eighty percent of women admit to having had sexual intercourse by the time they've reached twenty-one. Although most singles are including sex in their relationships, is this the wise thing to do?

The typical dating scenario I see goes like this: Scott and Jennifer meet. There is an attraction there and they decide to go out on a date. Jennifer thinks Scott is really handsome. Scott thinks Jennifer has a great body. They have fun on their date. A few days later, they go out again. They have another fun date. They seem to get along well so by the third date, Scott asks Jennifer to come back to his apartment with him. She gladly agrees. Over the next few months, they go out on lots of dates. Usually, they see the current movie and then go back to his place. After 3-4 months, Jennifer discovers that Scott is agnostic. Jennifer is very strong in her religious beliefs and can not imagine a long term relationship with someone who doesn't have the same beliefs. So the relationship ends and both are left with feelings of hurt and disappointment. You see, once they started having sex, they stopped getting to know each other.

For a great many people, having sex too early in a relationship can be the worst thing possible. Yes, I know that there's a tremendous temptation to just jump in when we first meet someone. The signals are right and the timing seems perfect, but if you make that move too quickly, you are going to find yourself in a position that is both precarious and relationship-ending.

In today's society, the issue isn't usually whether or not a couple is going to have sex before marriage, but when. At this point in time, it's becoming increasingly common for couples to have sex within the first few dates -- and it's not even uncommon on the first date.

For the moment, let's put aside the issues of morality and religious teachings. I'm not talking about abstaining until marriage. There are not going to be any judgments made about who you should have sex with or whether you should have sex before marriage or not.

I'm not here to pass judgment on you and I'm not here to try to convert you to my way of thinking.

I'm here to look at things from the viewpoint of what works and what doesn't in the overall relationship.

If we take a step back and look at things objectively, we can see common patterns in most relationships. We're here to find whether having sex early in a relationship actually strengthens or weakens it.

When you're looking for that special someone to spend the rest of your life with, will having sex early in the relationship make it more or less likely that you'll get married and stay married?

Or does having sex have any influence on the outcome of the relationship at all?

Like you, I've been involved in relationships where the sexual energy between me and my dating partner was so strong that it was practically an elemental force. We've all been with individuals who had us so enthralled that we can't even see straight. One of the concerns that I always had was whether or not it was the right time to move the relationship onto the next level. When do you move on to the sexual level in your relationships?

One of the reasons we need to think carefully about the right timing for sex is that it can bring an end to the relationship before it's even had a chance to start.

In our typical dating scenario Scott and Jennifer were just beginning to know each other. They knew just enough to determine there was a physical attraction between them. This is what is known as the "infatuation phase." During the first few dates, they were getting to know each other. But that came to a halt when they started having sex. The time they should have spent exchanging life stories was now being spent on having sex. I know you're thinking, what's wrong with that? Having sex is fun and exciting with a new partner. But this is time that should be spent on discussing likes and dislikes. Remember the list you made out in chapter 1? The first few dates are when you will spend time getting to know the other person so you can determine if they meet your requirements.

What happens once sex is introduced into the relationship is that the rose-colored relationship glasses are put on. The man and the woman are not seeing each other in terms of what might be a long-term relationship because they're caught up in the physical attraction of the moment. During this phase of the dating process, the two people are caught in the grip of powerful hormonal forces that emphasize positive aspects and turn a blind eye to some of the negative faults that could be uncovered.

This period can last from a few weeks to a few months, depending on the individuals. It's during the infatuation phase that some of the promises we've made to ourselves and some of the items we've put on our "must have" lists go out the window. That's because we're actually not thinking straight. We have other issues that are going through our minds. There's the excitement of a new relationship and the possibility of a new love. Because of these other issues, we're not focusing on what's important. We start to rationalize to ourselves. And then, something new is added into the equation.

Sex.

Through my work with many women and men, I've discovered one thing. It's something you need to understand to be successful in your relationships, and something that many people have not figured out.

Sex is a barrier to intimacy.

This might have you scratching your head, thinking, "Wait a minute. That doesn't make sense! How can sex be a barrier to intimacy? For one thing, having sex is called 'being intimate.'"

I'll admit that being naked with someone else involves a certain degree of intimacy. It can be very hard to bare our bodies to someone new. But sex is just physical intimacy. What we need to form a long lasting relationship with someone is emotional intimacy. Emotional intimacy comes from sharing feelings and ideas and hopes and dreams. It also includes sharing your anxieties and even sharing your fears. Emotional intimacy is much more difficult for most people than physical intimacy.

Sex has nothing to do with that.

Sex is just sex.

Many of us can look back on our past relationships and think about what once sex came into the picture. We realize that, most of the time, sex is what the relationship becomes about. Rather than being focused on getting to know each other better, the relationship becomes focused on the sex. Oh, sure, there are dates and going to movies. But during those times, what many people actually do is enter a kind of "sex" mode where the first part of the date is just killing time until they get to the sex. They're not making an effort to see if that person meets their requirements and wants. They're not asking any questions about what their date's hopes and dreams are or discovering whatever it is they want from life.

To give you an example, I've got a friend who is always in a relationship. Julie is either just starting a relationship, in the middle of a relationship, or just ending a relationship. Now, when she first starts out on a relationship, she's very "into" the other person and does whatever she can to find out who they are and what they're all about. However, once she begins to have sex with that person, the conversations cease. She switches over to a kind of "auto-pilot" relationship mode. It's as if she now feels that she's with this person so there's no longer any need to know them further. She knows them well enough to have sex, so there's no need to keep exploring. Unfortunately, what usually happens is that something comes up later down the line that causes a problem in the relationship. She didn't realize, or take the time to find out, that this was a part of her partner's personality, and the relationship will end.

That's why sex should never be entered into lightly. Let me add here that some people are not looking for a long term relationship. There are those who don't want to spend the time or effort trying to find that special someone at this point in their lives. For them, having sex can be a mere physical act that is enjoyable and has no strings attached. But that's not what we're talking about here. This book focuses on the vast majority of people who want to find a life partner, someone they can share the rest of their life with. For them, sex is more than a pleasurable pastime.

When we're in the dating process, the moment sex becomes part of the relationship; the whole "getting to know you" aspect comes to a screeching halt.

Why is that?

Again -- we've discussed this.

Sex is a barrier to intimacy.

Many of us think that sex is actually the highest form of intimacy. We've been told that a sexual relationship is the way to truly express you love and affection for your partner. So what that means for most of us is that when we start having sex, we automatically assume that we're being intimate There's nothing further that we need to do, nothing more that we need to know. After all, we've been with the other person in every way possible, and that means that we know everything there is to know about them. Besides, would you rather sit around talking for hours on end about politics and religion, or would you rather be having sex?

The reason having sex too soon can harm a relationship is because when we're in the infatuation stage, we're really not thinking clearly. Oh, sure, we might think our eyes are wide open. We're adults who are in charge of our own lives and we're scanning for telltale signs that will tell us whether or not we're with the person that we want to spend the rest of our lives with. We think we're being realistic about our date, but that's actually not the case. Instead, during the infatuation period, we have blinders on. That's because there are all kinds of changes taking place inside of us -- some on an emotional level and some on a physiological level.

Don't get me wrong. I'll be the first one to admit that having sex can be a thrilling prospect. Believe me, I've been down that road, so I know what it's like. What I'm telling you is that it's not a very good way to really get to know your partner or to decide whether or not they're the person that you want to spend the rest of your life with. The best way to get to know their heart and mind is to spend time talking, not having sex.

After a few months, the excitement begins to wear off. What once was new and different is now becoming routine and ordinary. That's when the flaws begin to appear. The funny thing is -- those flaws were always there. We just chose not to notice them. We chose not to get to know the person better before entering into the sex part of the relationship. That's the typical dating routine in our society these days. We are so thrilled at the prospect of having a new relationship that we want to hurry past the initial 'getting to know you' phase and go straight to the sexual relationship.

I usually see new clients when the excitement of the new sexual partner begins to wear thin. Things have been going great till now, they think. But suddenly problems begin to pop up in the relationship. This usually happens within the first 3-6 months. By this time, one or both partners are feeling an emotional attachment. That's because there's been a physical sharing -- what people are going to insist upon calling an "intimacy." This attachment is usually greater in women. Because of many physiological as well as emotional reasons, women just form an attachment more readily with someone than men, especially when sex is involved.

The trouble is, once the sexual excitement starts to wane, and once the fireworks start to fizzle out, one (and sometimes both) of the partners starts to realize that they really don't know the person that they've shared their bodies with. They've been dating someone for months, yet they don't even know the most basic things about them. And they hardly ever have had serious discussions where they share their hopes and dreams for the future.

In a worst case scenario, one or both partners will realize they don't like the person that they're with.

"I was involved with this one guy I met at a banquet," Barbara recalls, "and the two of us really hit it off. It seemed like we had so much in common. I decided that I was going to take it slow, because I'd been burned a couple of times before. So, we went out on a couple of dates, and I saw that he and I were really on the same wavelength. Well, one thing led to another, and before I knew it, we were sleeping together. At first, everything was really great. I don't think I was ever happier. But then, I started to notice little things about him. Things I didn't notice before. I was having a really hard time overlooking them now. Eventually I decided that the relationship really wasn't what I wanted, and I had to end it. It was really hard because the sex had always been great. But I knew that wasn't enough to overcome his personality traits that I didn't like. He kept calling me for days, until he finally got it through his head that it was over."

I'm sure you've known someone like Barbara and that you can relate to what she's saying. How many times have you seen someone enter a relationship and heard them say, "I'm going to take it slow," only to find them sleeping with their partner within a matter of days or weeks? Perhaps that's been you in previous relationships. We've all been there.

There's a myth out there that there's something called "casual sex." A lot of men and women are going under the misconception that everyone in the world is happy and carefree and having sex with no strings attached. Just turn on any television show and you'll be able to see that's how relationships are constantly being portrayed.

That's hardly the case, however.

Whether many of us want to admit the truth or not, we can't escape from the reality that "casual sex" is not the norm. Women have been told since the days of women's lib and bra burning that it's okay to have sex with anyone and everyone you choose. While that's a personal choice each of us must make, don't think you can do it and remain emotionally detached. Sure, there are people out there who can have sex and have absolutely no emotional strings attached to the other person, but they are the exception and not the rule. Instead, what usually happens when sex enters a relationship is that attachments are formed. It's also shown that when we feel an attachment to our partner, we automatically assume that our partner feels the same way. After all, they're having sex with us, right? Why wouldn't they be feeling the same things that we are?

Another important thing happens when sex enters the relationship picture. Everything is now changed. One or both parties assume that they are both going to stop dating other people. Suddenly, we've gone from a relationship to an EXCLUSIVE relationship.

Despite all the news reports about sexual freedom, most of us still will have only one sexual relationship at a time. This has been called serial monogamy. Serial monogamy means that once you enter into a sexual relationship with someone, you will only see that person. You will be true to them for as long as the relationship lasts. When that relationship is over, you will find another partner, and be faithful to them for as long as the new relationship lasts. So once we're dating someone and sex comes into play, our entire dating life comes to a halt.

Are you beginning to see why having sex too early in a relationship can be something less than desirable?

Let's remember that the ultimate goal of dating is to find the person we want to spend the rest of our life with. We're not going to be able to do that if we stop looking the moment that we have sex with someone and enter a relationship.

Let's look at the typical dating routine. You start dating someone and begin having sex early on in your dating. You then stop dating others because you don't want to 'cheat' on your partner. This goes on for several months and things are fine. You start thinking that maybe this one will work out better than the last one. But after 3-6 months you begin to notice things that really bother you about your partner. If you are smart enough to check your list of requirements and wants, you see that not all of your requirements are there, and certainly not all of your wants. You spend the next 6 months trying to make him become the person you want him to be. When that doesn't work, you spend the next six months trying to convince yourself that you can change and that your requirements aren't really requirements. Finally, you decide it's just not going to work for you. You have to end it. Both you and your partner are emotionally distraught by the end of another relationship and the prospect of starting the whole thing over yet again.

This whole process usually takes 1-2 years. Let's be kind and say it was only one year. If you immediately enter into another relationship, you can date 1 person per year. If you do that every year from the time you're 18 till you're 30, you've only dated twelve different men! TWELVE MEN! Do you think you can find the right one by only dating twelve men? Perhaps you can, but your chances would be much greater if you dated 50 men, or 100 men. If you're shopping for a new party dress, are you going to look in just one store and choose something from that store no matter what? They have a great selection of party dresses. But you wouldn't buy one from that store if they didn't have one the right color or the right size. You'd search through hundreds of dresses in many stores to find just the right one.

You should do the same thing when shopping for a man. Your search for your life partner should entail at least the same thought and energy you would spend on finding the right dress. The current way of dating wastes a lot of your time and severely limits your chances of finding someone who is right for you.

"What if I have sex with someone, but they understand that I'm still going to be dating other people?" you might ask.

I had a friend who thought he could manage to pull that off.

Do you want to know what happened?

At first, things were okay with him and the partner he was dating. He was having sex with her, and he was also dating other women in his quest to find the one person he wanted to spend the rest of his life with.

This lasted for all of three days. Then he and his partner had a huge fight and that was the end of it.

Later on, when we were talking about what had happened, he was genuinely confused.

"She said she was all right with it," he told me. "But it turned out that she really wasn't."

What really surprised me was that he was actually caught off-guard by this. Now, I know that he should have had a better understanding of human nature, but the fact is that even if your partner is willing to sign a legal agreement telling you that they are okay with you dating other people, they are wrong. There will come a time in the relationship when they will put their foot down and say, "Either you stop seeing everyone else or I'm going to have to break up with you." The thought of having a relationship including sex with someone just doesn't go with dating multiple people. Even most men would admit that they would not stay in a relationship with someone who was also seeing others, especially if their partner was having sex with others as well.

Some of you might be thinking that when you start having sex in a relationship, you might have found the person you're going to be with for the rest of your life.

It's possible. There will always be couples who meet, have sex on the first date, and have a long, happy marriage.

Unfortunately, it's highly unlikely.

Take a look at the list you wrote and study it. Think about the person you're considering having sex with. Match that person with what's on the list. Do they meet all of your requirements? The odds are that you probably haven't even learned enough about them to know whether or not they are compatible. You don't know them well enough, at this point to be able to determine if they meet all your requirements. You certainly don't know about the wants. You want to sleep with them, but you're not even sure if they match most of the requirements on your list.

That's not a good sign.

That's why it's so important that you allow yourself the freedom of parallel dating. Parallel dating will allow you to get to know potential partners better in the beginning. You will be able to 'weed out' the one's who are not right for you more quickly so you can spend more time looking for the one's who are more suitable.

Let's go back to the current way of dating. The typical monogamous relationship lasts six to twelve months. That relationship ends and it takes you a few months to find another relationship that you want to try out. Right there, we're looking at about one year per relationship.

Ten relationships in ten years.

That's a scary thought. During the time when most of us are looking for a life partner and wanting to get married, during our 20's, we are only going to have ten relationships. What's even scarier is that most people, once they've been through 3-5 relationships, start to think about making the commitment. They've actually only been in relationships with a handful of people, but they are thinking about making a commitment that could last the remainder of their lives. It seems a little absurd that you would make a lifetime commitment based on only a few different relationships. But if you only date a dozen different people, each one becomes more important. If you're on relationship number 8, for example, you're getting older and start to think you may be running out of options. If you are ever going to be married, you'd better do it quick.

That's absolutely mind-boggling.

Many people will get married after dating just three or four people. Do you think that this might explain why nearly half of all people who get married this year will wind up in divorce court?

"What about someone who's already been married, though?" you might ask. "Aren't they more likely to avoid making a serious mistake?"

Gee, you'd think so, wouldn't you? You would think that we'd learn from our first mistake and make a better choice the second time around. Unfortunately, statistics show that that second marriages actually have a failure rate of about 65%. They fail more often than first marriages.

It gets even worse with the third marriage.

Couples who marry for the third time have a 75% chance of becoming unmarried again.

Talk about a sobering statistic.

You've just seen why holding off on having sex early in the relationship isn't a moral or a religious issue. Clearly, in order to have the best possible success rate of finding the right person, you need to keep sex out of the picture -- at least, until well into the whole dating process.

And don't think that being a parallel dater makes you any kind of slut or gigolo. Nothing could be further from the truth. What you're doing is taking an intelligent and practical approach to finding the person you want to spend the rest of your life with. It may not seem as romantic as hopping into bed at the first signs of passion, but it will help you get what you want. Remember, you can have sex with just about anyone. You don't want to spend the rest of your life with just anyone though. You want to find someone who meets your relationship requirements; someone who is compatible in mind and spirit, and not just sexually.

There's nothing wrong with that.

As it becomes known that you're single and available, you're going to be presented with the opportunities to meet a great many people. Let your friends and family know you are looking for a partner. Your coworkers can be a great source. Network with them and don't be afraid to date several people at once. By implementing a parallel dating system, you'll find that you have a choice of a number of potential partners, and you'll also find yourself able to quickly eliminate anyone who doesn't meet what you're looking for.

If you're serious about parallel dating -- and if you are sincere in what you are looking for --

you'll find that you're able to meet and date many potential partners in just a few months.

That means your odds of finding someone to spend the rest of your life with are a whole lot better than if you were a "serial dater." You can spend time getting to know each date without the pressure of thinking time is running out for you.

So, you meet someone and you seem to hit it off. Fine, you can go out on your first date.

If things seem to be going nicely, you can go out on a second and third date.

At this point, you'll begin to know whether or not you want this to continue. With some experience, you can usually know after just a few dates if that person meets your relationship requirements. If they meet your requirements, you'll want to continue dating to see if they also match most of your wants and niceties. This will take longer to discover. If they don't meet your requirements, the best thing to do is to stop dating them. You can part as friends without all the emotional distress because you have not had sex. No bond has formed yet which makes the parting easier on both parties. Remember we're talking about finding your life partner. If you want to date just for fun and are not serious about finding a partner, that's okay. Just be sure the person you're dating understands this as well. Don't string someone along just because you like their company. If you decide they do not fit your partner profile and know you could never enter into a serious relationship with them, it's easier to stop the dating process early.

By following the parallel dating regime, you'll soon develop a group of people that you're serious about dating. It's still okay to date more than one.

This is where you should really start getting to know them.

By this, I'm talking about really getting to know them. I want you to take sex right out of the picture. You do not need to think about heading there, at this point in time.

This is the point where you're sharing your life stories, talking about your hopes and dreams. This is also the point where you're being brutally honest. Remember -- what you're trying to do here is find out whether or not you're with someone that you may want to spend the rest of your life with. There's no point in being dishonest now just to try to impress your date. As the relationship progresses, the truth will eventually come out. Then you will have ruined a potentially great relationship just because you were trying to impress them.

At this point of the dating process, you'll be able to tell whether or not this person is going to "climb the ladder" of what you're looking for. You'll get a sense as to whether or not they are potential long term material.

If they turn out to be passing muster, you continue with the process.

However, if it turns out that they are lacking in too many areas, it's time to terminate it. If you determine, at any point, that they are not the one you're looking for you can end the dating process and move on. It's never easy to end a relationship, even a beginning one. But it's much easier to end it if there's no sexual component than if you've been having sex for several months. And you won't experience the guilt many women feel after ending yet another sexual relationship. Despite all our sexual freedom and women's lib, most women still don't like the idea of having multiple sexual partners. Even if it's just one at a time, they don't like the thought of accumulating 10-20 different sex partners.

When you stop dating one person, you now have free time to start dating someone else. You will have to decide how much time each week you can devote to the dating process. It's entirely up to you. Some women want to go out every night of the week. Some limit their dates to weekends only. This is important because you don't want to get booked up with one individual. Make sure you leave time open and available for others. This is another common error women make. They end up in an exclusive relationship with someone not because they think he may be the right one for them, but because they allow him to occupy all their free dating time. If you only want to date on weekends, don't book up next weekend with the same guy you're out with now. Just because he's asked you out again you don't have to make a commitment right away. Keep some time open to see someone else. This may mean that you'll spend some weekends by yourself. But if you allow yourself to get booked up with one person, you'll never have time to meet anyone new.

My friend, Lara, began dating a man several years ago. I'll call him Harry. Harry was really fun to be with. He took her to expensive restaurants and bought her nice presents. Because of her job, Lara could only date on weekends. She went out with Harry several weekends in a row. He would always have something fun planned. They would go to a concert, the ballgame, a friend's party. But Lara knew Harry was not right for her. There were some big issues, such as children and religion, they did not agree on. But Lara allowed Harry to occupy all her dating time. While they were out on a date, he would talk about what they would do the next weekend. It always sounded like so much fun that Lara couldn't refuse. This went on for almost a year. Lara lamented the fact that she never met anyone else. "If I met someone else I wanted to date, I wouldn't go out with Harry any more," she said. She thought going out and having fun with Harry was better than sitting home alone. Turns out it isn't. If all your dating time is spent with one person you will never be able to begin dating anyone else. You may as well be having sex and be in an exclusive relationship. At least then you can enjoy the sex.

As you gain more experience in parallel dating you will become more adept at it. It will take you less time to decide if someone has the potential to be a good partner for you or not. Soon it will become obvious that you've got a favorite among your dating circle. Once you've found a favorite, it's time to consider moving on to the next step.

I'll give you a hint -- it's not marriage.

Avoid the common mistake of having sex too soon in your relationship by parallel dating. Take more time in the beginning getting to know someone before you give in to your passions. By taking your time at the start, you won't be wasting your time with someone who is not right for you.

Chapter Five

Mistake #4

Becoming Exclusive Too Soon

Ⅰf you look around at the today's society, you'll see that things have gotten much more organized than they've ever been before. We all have routines that we are settled into, and we all have various structures that are a part of our lives. This is because the world today is much more fast-paced, more frantic. In order to function well, it's important to have a routine. We all need a workable system to keep our lives organized and on track.

One of the most important business models to appear on the scene in the past ten years is the "networking" concept. At its most basic, networking deals with groups of like-minded individuals who work together to support each other. When you network, you let others know what you want or need. If they can help you, great! But the best part is that even if they can't help you directly, they may know someone who can. By doing this you essentially expand your pool of acquaintances and have a better chance of getting the help you need.

You can also apply this concept to dating. By networking with your friends you are not merely relying on bumping in to the right person yourself, but expanding your odds by having friends scouting for you as well. If your friends know what you are looking for, they may meet someone who could be right for you. They can make the introduction and you're on your way. Unfortunately, many people don't even think about networking as a way to expand their likelihood of finding the right partner. For some reason, a great many people still think that the best way to find their future partner is to use a haphazard "hit or miss" approach. I don't understand this thinking, especially by today's techno-savvy women. Rather than going out there and networking with our friends and business associates, we wait for dates to come to us. We don't think we can apply the same networking system to our dating plan as we would to our business plan.

But most women sit at home alone. They keep waiting for someone to come along and somehow magically appear. You might consider this the "Prince Charming" approach. You're just waiting for the right man to come along.

He'll be handsome, and dazzling, and perfect. He'll sweep you off your feet and take you in his arms, and the two of you will escape from your boring life to a new life filled with adventure and excitement and eternal bliss. Somehow, you'll live happily ever after.

How's that working out for you so far? Women who are normally outgoing and vivacious suddenly become wallflowers when it comes to dating. When you take this passive approach to dating, you'll have a lot fewer choices available to you. How many new people do you meet in a week? If you're like most of us, probably not very many. So your odds are not very good that you'll randomly meet someone who could be your future partner. You'll also find that your dates are chosen by someone else. Rather than you choosing who you want to go out with, someone else is choosing – it's your dates.

The only people that you'll date are the men who find and approach you. Until the man just happens to meet you somehow, you sit at home and wait for the phone to ring. Now, if you're a woman who is waiting for the right man to just come along, you might think that there aren't many available men out there. After all, you've been available for quite a while, and there haven't been a lot of men approaching you. So, that obviously means that there aren't all that many men out there. It's common for women to feel that way.

This is when you start to feel a little desperate. There aren't that many men out there and you're getting older by the minute. It only stands to reason that time might be running out for you. This is destructive thinking. When you think this way, when you get the seeds of desperation inside of you, you let yourself be vulnerable. You are so anxious to find a man that whoever pays attention to you will be the one you stay with. Many women do this and find themselves settling for someone they don't really care for. It's the same old 'any man is better than no man' attitude. They don't want to spend the rest of their lives with just the dog. So they get a little frantic.

So here's what usually happens. You go out on a date with a man for two or three times. You had a good time and he's attractive enough that you want to go out with him again. Then something begins to happen inside of your head. You start to think of yourself as part of a couple.

In my relationship coaching practice, I've listened to women who have dated a man once or twice, and all of a sudden, they don't want to date anyone else. They feel that if a man is good enough to date two or three times, he is probably going to be marriage material -- and this is only after a couple of dates! You probably know women like this. Maybe you are one of those women. I'm telling you that you can't possibly know after just a couple of dates whether or not the man is a good match for you. You just can't get to know someone enough in that short a time.

So you're thinking that you don't want to date anyone else; that you and he are a pair. But how do you know if he's thinking the same thing? Perhaps he has a different point of view.

For starters, most men aren't ready to "settle down" after the first couple of dates. In fact, that's probably the furthest thing from the man's mind. He's just found someone that he likes being with, and that's about as far as his thinking goes. You may even have started having sex, but remember that doesn't mean you're a couple. But, if you were to ask a man when the wedding is going to be after just a few dates, he'll look at you like you've grown two heads. Some women, though, are already picking out their wedding dress after the third date. They already think of themselves and their man as a couple.

Right away we have a problem in the relationship. The woman is thinking about being exclusive at this point -- and she's assuming that the man wants to be exclusive as well. Needless to say, few couples actually talk about. The woman is just making the assumption that because she wants to be exclusive, the man must be thinking the same thing. This is even more common if the couple is having sex. Most women assume having sex means they are going to be exclusive. (Remember from a previous chapter, men don't see it that way). My experience is that most men are not thinking the same thing. They're thinking that their new woman is fun to be with and they want to take her out again, but they're not ready to exclude everyone else yet.

Dear Kathy,

I'm 23 years old and I'm in a relationship with a guy I love very much. We've been seeing each other for six months. The problem is he recently told me that he has another girlfriend and I don't know what to do now because I can't end it. I'm in love with the guy. Also, there's another guy who says he loves me. I think I love him too, but I'm just confused.

Andrea

Dear Andrea,

Why can't you date both guys to find out which one (if either) you love? The problem is that you think you're in a relationship with the first guy and that you two are exclusive. Obviously your guy doesn't see it that way. If you've not made an agreement not to date others, you really shouldn't be surprised that he's seeing someone else as well. There's no need to stop seeing him altogether, but there's no reason why you can't see others too. Date both of them until you get to know them well enough to determine if either will be a good match for you. Then talk to your guy about dating exclusively before you decide to do it on your own.

Andrea's case shows what happens when women assume that because they've been out with someone a few times they are in an exclusive relationship. Women just don't seem to be able to date many men at a time. They want a relationship and they're going to have it whether the man knows what's going on or not.

There is no conversation about being exclusive. It's not even mentioned. As far as the man knows, he and the woman are just dating, just seeing where things lead. It never occurs to him that it is time to start being exclusive. You know what happens next. He's still dating other women and thinking everything is fine. Then the first woman finds out he's dating others and she's crushed. She thinks they have an exclusive relationship and he's cheating on her.

All of a sudden, there's a huge battle taking place in the relationship and he has no idea where this came from. He thought they were getting along great and having a good time together. In fact, the first thing that a man will usually say when a woman confronts him about dating someone else is, "What are you getting so upset about? We never said that we weren't going to see anyone else."

The woman is now really angry. She says, "I didn't think we had to spell it out. I just assumed that you felt the same way I did. I thought you knew we were exclusive." At this point the relationship is usually doomed. Since she wants to be exclusive and he doesn't, it's just not going to work out. If they had talked about it before the big blow-up, however, they could have come to an understanding and perhaps gotten to the point of being exclusive sometime in the future. But once this big argument takes place it's extremely hard to continue the relationship.

Let's talk some more about the sex part of the equation. We discussed this in a previous chapter, but it's really important for you to remember. To most men, having sex does not mean you are dating exclusively. It just means you are having sex. But women think that if they are having sex with someone, he's not going to see anyone else. They usually will not date anyone else once they begin a sexual relationship with a man, so they assume he will not either. Despite what some recent attitudes reflected in the media happen to be, most women are not promiscuous. Having sex leads them to think of the relationship as exclusive, that means they start to think of it as a "long term" relationship. From there, thoughts turn to marriage and a permanent relationship.

One client called me very upset. Her boyfriend of one year had just broken up with her. She was devastated. Here's what happened: They started out the usual way. They dated several times and really hit it off. After just a few weeks, they were having sex. From that point on, she didn't see anyone else. She assumed that he wasn't either, but they never discussed it. They saw each other practically every weekend. She thought he could be the one for her. They even discussed her moving in with him. If that worked out well, she thought, they would talk about marriage. The past couple of months, however, he had been more distant. He was complaining about little things she did, things that's she'd always done. He never complained about them before. The night before he called and told her that he didn't think it was going to work and they had to break up. When she asked why, he said that she was getting too serious and he just wasn't ready for that. He was happy the way things were but she was starting to get too serious and he didn't want that. She was totally surprised.

But, you see, they never talked about dating exclusively. She just assumed he wanted the same thing she did. Once they started having sex, the whole thing progressed from there in her mind, but not in his.

You see, on some level (and it might even be subconscious), the woman introduces sex into the picture. This is because she's already thinking that she's in a long-term relationship. Now, if you're a typical man and the woman that you're dating decides that she wants to take the relationship to the next level, do you really think that you're going to turn down sex? Most men will not refuse to have sex if the woman is offering.

At this point, however, the woman is engaged in a kind of self-delusion. In her head, the relationship is serious and exclusive and long-term. That's why the sex is okay. However, the man hasn't been let into the loop on this little fact. He has no idea that having sex with the woman is all part of this huge romantic fantasy that she's created. It's just sex with someone he likes. It may lead to something more in the future. But men don't have everything planned out in their heads like women do. They take things more slowly and stay in the moment.

As we've mentioned before, this practice of dating one man at a time is called serial monogamy. That's when a woman will date a man for a few times and then see him exclusively. She'll convince herself that he's "The One." Sometimes, the relationship they're in will last for weeks or months or even years. At some point, however, she's going to open her eyes and decide that this isn't the man that she wants to spend the rest of her life with. Unfortunately, she's wasted valuable time in coming to this realization. The opportunity cost of engaging in serial monogamy is tremendously high.

You see, if the woman had taken her time in the beginning of the relationship to weed out the men that she wasn't going to see herself having a long-term relationship with, she could have moved onto the next man more quickly. For most women, I would think that dating between ten and thirty men in a twelve-month period would result in the best results for finding the man that is just right for her. How many women do you know who do this? And the ones who do are usually thought of as being 'loose'.

Keep in mind we're not saying that a woman has to sleep with ten to thirty men in a year in order to find the right guy.   This isn't about sex. It's about finding a man who meets your requirements.   It's about finding someone to spend the rest of your life with.

With some practice, most women will be able to eliminate some of those men after one date or two dates. That's why it's so important for a woman to be honest about what she's looking for in a man. She must be clear about what is going to constitute a "deal breaker" for her. The sooner she is able to take some of the wrong men out of the picture, the more likely it's going to be that she'll find the right man.

Think of a relationship as a motion picture and you're the director. You're casting a part for the "perfect man." Now, as a director, are you just going to wait for one or two men to trickle along to try out for the part? Of course not. You won't sit in your office and hope the right one will drop by somehow.

You're going to have a casting call, and you're going to have as many people read for the part as possible. Otherwise, you'd find yourself hiring the first guy that came along that was "somewhat" right for the part. You may even start filming, only to get halfway through and find out this isn't the right guy, after all. At that point, you'd have someone else read for the part, you'd hire them, and you'd go through the whole process again. No way.

We're talking about your life here and your happiness. This means that you've got to get serious about what you're looking for. And you have to have a plan as to how you're going find it.

The days when you can afford to just be exclusive with one person and hope that you've found the right one are long gone. As we can see from the ever increasing numbers of divorces, that routine doesn't work.   It's time that you took a more proactive approach, and that means that you're going to have to engage in something that is new and different.

This is where parallel dating comes in. I know this is a new and seemingly strange concept to most of you, but you have to admit that what we've been doing doesn't work very well. I'm talking here about dating more than one man at a time. Why not date two or three or even four men at the same time? You could date Frank on Monday, Kevin on Friday, and Jake on Saturday. These are social get-togethers that we're talking about here. They're simple little dates so that you have the opportunity to get to know them better and they have the opportunity to get to know you.

They are not excuses for casual sex. We're not making a judgment about when and who you should have sex with. Just remember, women have a very hard time separating sex and commitment.   They are not "two-dates-and-we're-a-couple" events.

They are just dates. You might wonder what happens if Frank finds out about Kevin. So what? You're just dating these guys. You're trying to find the right person for you. You're not going to do that if you tie yourself down to one person and wait months before you can eliminate him and move on to the next one on your list. Just make sure you don't promise to date one exclusively or lead them to think that you're not seeing anyone else. You don't want to lie to them.

And, if you find that one of your potential partners is getting overly jealous or overly attached, perhaps he's not the partner that you want to spend the rest of your life with. This is part of the getting to know them.

Let's say that you want to buy a house. Buying a house is a big investment, and you're not going to just walk into the first house you see, put down your money, and take out a 20-year mortgage, are you? No, of course you wouldn't. You're going to go through that house and check it out completely. Then you're also going to see what other houses are available that might be what you're looking for.

If you take the time to find the right house for you, why in the world wouldn't you take the time to find the right man for you, as well? The good news with parallel dating is that you'll know, usually within the first couple of dates, whether or not you want to continue seeing a man. It's a lot easier to end a potential relationship early on in the dating cycle, rather than later. If you've gone out with someone a few times and decide he's not right for you, you can stop seeing him and maybe even remain friends. Especially if you have not begun a sexual relationship, it's a lot easier on both of you. Ending a relationship with someone you've had sex with is always difficult whether you're the one who decides to end it or not.

In addition, as you date more men, you'll learn more things about yourself. You'll be interacting with more and more people, and you'll get a better sense of what it is that you like and what it is that you dislike. For example, you might tell yourself, "I don't like sushi," even though you've never tried it. Then, one day, you taste it, and you discover that you actually do like it.

The same thing holds true for different men. You might tell yourself, "I don't want someone who is too serious," but you might find someone who is very serious -- and yet, still manages to have a playful side. This is someone that you might not even have given a chance to begin with, had you not decided to parallel date and uncovered new aspects about yourself.

Now, as you go through the parallel dating process, you'll find that you're crossing off more and more men. Remember, though -- when you eliminate someone as a potential mate, that frees up some time for you to add someone else to it.

At some point, you'll to discover that one or two men are standing out from everyone else. When this happens, you can focus on these two men for a few more dates. If one man stands out from the rest after several months, you may begin to think about seeing him more and seeing others less.

This very well might be the man that you've been looking for your entire life. We're not sure about that yet, but it's a distinct possibility. However, before you start sending out wedding invitations, it's time for you and him to have "The Discussion."

When you're having The Discussion, you need to be honest with your feelings. This is not the time to play games. You tell this man that you're attracted to him and that you'd like to continue to date him. If he agrees, you explain that you will stop dating other men, and you'd like him to stop dating other women. It's important that you spell these things out. You're trying to avoid any misunderstandings about this in the future. You may think that you shouldn't have to be so obvious, but you do. Nothing hurts more than to think you are in an exclusive relationship only to find out your man doesn't think so.

Once you both agree not to date others, the two of you are now exclusive. Notice that I said you both agreed. That means the man is doing this because he wants to, not because you've pressured him into it, and not because you threatened to stop seeing him if he didn't agree. It's his choice of his own free will. However, the two of you are still not committed.

What exclusive means is that you've agreed to spend your dating time only each other, so that the dating process can be accelerated. It means that the two of you see the potential in the relationship and you're interested in going further with it. However, it also means that because neither of you are committed, you can leave the relationship if you find someone that you like better, or if you decide that he isn't "The One," after all.

What about sex? I've said before that women should delay having sex in their relationship. Now would be the time to introduce that aspect if you want. That's entirely up to you. However, don't make the assumption that because you're having sex, it means he's going to want to marry you or to spend the rest of his life with you. It just means that you're both still learning about each other and trying to determine if you are a good match. A sexual relationship can be part of that, but doesn't have to be. It's your choice and your decision.

How long should you be in the exclusive part of the relationship? Personally, I recommend a year. I think twelve months of getting to truly know another person is the minimum time investment that you should make. You might want to take longer, and that's certainly fine. Everyone has their own time table for this. What I want you to be clear on is that one year is the least amount of time you need to be sure if someone is right for you. That's one year before you think about making a commitment.

After that, it's time to have "The Commitment Talk." This is where you and he are sharing your feelings about possible commitment to each other. You should know each other well enough to decide whether you want to continue dating, or if you want to spend the rest of your life with each other. If you both agree that you want to spend your lives together, that's when you decide to commit to each other...and to commit to the relationship.

The important thing about committing to a relationship is that you're taking an honest and intelligent look at the situation. Let's face it -- there are no guarantees out there. No one can promise you that everything is going to be smooth and trouble-free. Every relationship has it's good times and not so good times.

What you can do, however, is know that when things are rough, you're committed to working it out. You don't have to know how you're going to manage that. The only thing you have to do is know that you are going to stick it through, and that you're not going to disappear at the first sign of trouble. More importantly, you know that your partner is not going to disappear at the first sign of trouble.

It's important to really think things through at this stage of the relationship. You and your partner have now seen a lot of each other — enough to know whether or not you want even more to continue. You've invested time and effort and energy into the relationship. However, that doesn't mean that you automatically have to commit. If there's something inside you that says this still isn't right, you don't have to continue with it, just because you've already put in a tremendous effort.

The whole point of doing all this is to find the one who is right for you — not marry someone just because you've been dating exclusively for a year or more.

Don't make the same mistake many women make of being exclusive too soon. Take more time in the beginning of your dating to get to know people better before you take yourself off the dating market. This will greatly increase you chances of finding someone who is right for you. It will also help you avoid wasting years on a relationship that was not right from the beginning.

None of us can predict the future. When we get into a relationship, we have no idea what happiness or what sadness lies ahead of us. But, when you're committed to another person, when you stand before witnesses and take your wedding vows, you have the knowledge that the relationship is on solid ground. Yes, there are going to be times when there's a storm coming and you might have to weather it as best you can. But you'll do that -- because you and your partner are committed to getting through it...together.

Chapter Six

Mistake #5

Assuming He's Committed

Women crave commitment and men avoid it. Isn't that what we all believe? In fact, if you take a good look at our society, you'll see that it's practically become a cliché. Unfortunately, the reason clichés get started is because there is some truth to them.

I've seen this firsthand. My friend Christina was always looking for a relationship. She really wanted to get married and have a family of her own. When I say she was looking, though, I don't mean she was testing the waters. She wasn't surveying the dating landscape. No, that gal was on a mission. She was looking for commitment. The moment she dated someone-as soon as they said goodnight on their first date and kissed the first time-Christina was expecting an exclusive relationship and soon a committed one.

On the other hand, my friend Rick is the exact opposite. He's a habitual dater. He is in perpetual "date" mode. Not only is he not looking for commitment, he avoids it. It doesn't matter if he's on his first date or his tenth date -- the man simply doesn't want to admit that there may be anything more than dating.

Even though both of my friends might seem like they are walking clichés, the truth is that commitment is what many women are looking for the moment they decide to date someone. For men, the whole concept of commitment is something they just can't wrap their minds around. Why should they make a commitment to one woman when there are so many out there?

But, for the majority of us there is a middle ground. Despite the clichés, the reality is that both men and women are looking for a committed relationship at some point in their lives. The timing varies from person to person, but eventually, both men and women want to settle down with one partner for the long term. Both men and women grow tired of dating. They look at their relationship and decide that they want something more out of it. They want something that is permanent and lasting.

What's the problem, then?

The problem arises because men and women define commitment differently. When it comes to women, commitment in a relationship means stability and permanence. It means you're only seeing one person. In most cases, women assume that when they're having sex with someone, there's some kind of commitment. Or they assume that because they're in an exclusive relationship, there's a commitment.

But ask the man if he's in a committed relationship and you may get a totally different answer. Men look at the issue of commitment differently.

First of all, it's important to understand that most men want to be in committed relationships. They really do. They might not want it right now, but they definitely want it someday. Remember that over 90% of all young adults say their ideal is to get married and stay married to the same person for their entire life. Many women and men enter second and third marriages because they want a long term, committed relationship. Sure, we've all heard the myths about the man who will go to any length possible to avoid commitment, but for the vast majority of men, something like that simply isn't true.

The problem comes in when you ask a man to define a committed relationship.

You see, most women go around assuming that because a man is having sex with them, or because a man is not dating anyone else, they are in a committed relationship. If you ask the men that they're involved with if they're in a committed relationship, though, the men will tell you that they're not.

For most men, having sex is not a sign of commitment. It's just sex. Also, dating one woman exclusively is not a sign of commitment. I know that this is going to upset a lot of women, but it's the truth.

The sooner we face the truth about the differences between men and women, the sooner we can resolve the differences between the sexes so that each partner understands the other better. The goal is for both partners to get what they want in a relationship.

To women, commitment is very much like reciting marriage vows. When they feel that they are in a committed relationship, they are thinking all about "for better and for worse, in sickness and in health, etc." When a woman finds herself in a committed relationship, she's thinking that the relationship is going to last forever. She and her current partner may not be married yet, but someday they will be. Unless something unforeseen happens, she is ready to think about marriage and all the responsibilities that come with it.

Women get the definition right although they mess up the application. Women want the stability and security of a committed relationship so badly that they will commit to a man when they shouldn't. Women make commitments without shopping around and without getting to fully know their partners. You may criticize men for being shallow and being attracted by a woman's physical assets, but consider that many women are willing to commit to a man who has a pulse and a paycheck. If a man pays attention and flatters a woman, that's good enough for her. That's just as shallow, but in a different way. By committing too soon in a relationship, women set themselves up for relationship remorse later down the road. Like after they've had several babies and finally decide they can't take it anymore. Further, a lot of women want their fantasy wedding. In fact, it's more than a want: they deserve it. Oh, the pageantry of it all! The flowers, the beautiful wedding dress, the woman as the center of the universe. Since the wedding follows from commitment, they naturally want to get committed as soon as possible to start the whole wedding thing.

Believe it or not, most men understand commitment. Their definition is pretty much the same as women's. In fact, maybe men have a better grasp of what it means to be committed than do women. Maybe, their reluctance to make a commitment is the result of their knowing all to well what's at stake. Commitment is, by definition, a permanent situation. So perhaps men are really smarter about making a commitment than are the women. What seems like avoidance strategy for men is actually their unwillingness to enter into a permanent relationship until they are really, really sure. Women could learn from that.

Did you know that most divorces are initiated by women? Putting aside the reasons for a divorce, what if the reason for the woman's initiating the divorce is because of her relationship remorse-remorse caused by committing too soon? Maybe if women also postponed commitment until they were really, really sure there might be less relationship remorse and fewer divorces.

Here is the real issue: women commit too soon because of all the perceived benefits of a committed relationship. And because they want the committed relationship so badly, they assume the man wants the same commitment at the same time. The man doesn't want to upset the woman, so he says nothing to correct her thinking. Furthermore, since most men have less well developed communication skills than do women, a man often finds it difficult to verbalize what he really feels. It's easier just to say nothing.

When a man says nothing about an issue, it does not mean he agrees with you. If you believe the two of you are a committed couple, but he says nothing in agreement, you should not assume he is committed. If a man is truly committed he will say or do something to confirm it. But most women take a man's silence as agreement and, therefore, as commitment. A man can have sex with you without being committed to you. A man can live with you without being committed to you. A man can get you pregnant and not be committed to you.

Write this down and post it on your refrigerator: when a man is dating you exclusively but does nothing to declare his commitment, he is really telling you that he will stay with you until someone better comes along.

When he is committed to you, his talk and his behavior will leave no doubt. He will take positive action to let the world know of his commitment. The most common way for him to do that is with a ring and a date.

There's another aspect to commitment. You're smart enough to know that even though you're in a committed relationship, things are going to occasionally be rough and rocky. That's why the wedding vows include the words "for better or worse." There is no perfect couple out there, and there is no relationship that is going to sail along without hitting some turbulent seas occasionally.

That's why commitment is about more than your partner. Commitment is also about the relationship.

When you're in a committed relationship, you should do more than just commit to your partner. You should consciously acknowledge that you're going to make the relationship work. This is where a lot of women make serious mistakes. They think that just because they're committed to their partner they're going to have an easy time with the relationship. If you love each other, what else do you need?

Sounds pretty reasonable, doesn't it? But we all know that every relationship is going to have some ups and downs. Men are also reasonable creatures, so they should feel the same way. But let's take a look at how men view commitment.

Oddly enough, men share pretty much the same view of commitment as women do. When they make a commitment, they intend to keep that commitment for life. The problem shows up when a man's view of what constitutes being in a committed relationship differs from that of a woman.

You see, most women automatically assume that when they've have exclusive sex with a man they are in a committed relationship. How many times has this happened to you? You date someone a few times. After you start having sex, you don't want to see anyone else. After all, you're not promiscuous. Since you're dating only one man, you assume you're in a committed relationship. Unfortunately, the guy has not been informed of this little fact. The two of you have never discussed it. You didn't need to discuss it, right? You just KNEW you were both exclusive. And too often you assumed that you were both committed. That leads to big problems down the road.

For men, having sex with a woman has nothing to do with feeling commitment. Like it or not, it's important to understand that men don't even have to particularly like a woman in order to have sex with her.

That's why it is important for all of the women out there to understand this.

> *Almost without exception, men in exclusive relationships do not automatically consider themselves committed.*

So, what does exclusive mean to men? If you're dating one guy and he's only dating you, and the two of you are having sex, you have a committed relationship, right? How can a guy not understand that he's in a committed relationship?

It's easy. When it comes to women, exclusive means, "I am with you now, and I'm going to be with you forever." They equate exclusive to a commitment.

When it comes to men, exclusive means, "I am with you now, and I'm going to be with you until someone better comes along."

I know it's a hard thing to accept that a man is in a relationship with you and he's only in it until someone better comes along. But, the truth is this is the reality with most men. Just because you want to have a committed relationship doesn't make it so. A man can be happy dating only you, but he's still looking. If he sees someone else he'd like to date, he will end your relationship and start another. At least let's give men credit where credit is due. Most men will end their current relationship before pursuing a new one. Even men remain exclusive and only see one woman at a time.

Do you see where the problems in relationships come in? The man and the woman are involved with each other, possibly only having sex with each other, but they never actually had a conversation about the relationship and where it was going.

That's not a good thing. It leaves a lot of room open for assumptions and hurt feelings later on.

Now, this might seem like men actually don't want commitment in a relationship, but that's not true. Men do want commitment, but they generally take longer to want it.

In other words, men and women have different lengths of time to reach the point in their relationship where they decide that they want to commit to one another.

This is illustrated in the whole dating cycle. You will start dating a man. In many cases, within a few dates, you'll have sex with him. Now, within those few dates -- and definitely by the time sex comes into the picture – you're looking for the relationship to be exclusive. You're not going to be having sex with multiple men. You will not date anyone else as long as you're still seeing this man.

But, in the dating process, two problems usually occur in the early stages.

The first problem is that the guy is going to want sex, and the woman might not. Maybe she's not sure if she wants to date only him. But she risks losing him if she doesn't agree. So she may agree because she likes him and wants to see if the relationship will grow, or she may agree because she doesn't want to risk never seeing him again. After the couple does have sex, the woman wants the relationship to be exclusive. This is perfectly natural.

The man, however, may not have the same understanding. To a man, having sex and being exclusive don't necessarily go hand-in-hand. If he doesn't want to date only her, the woman feels like she's being used.

This leads to another problem in the relationship.

She thinks that because he wanted to have sex with her, he must really like her. At this point, the woman is usually thinking that the man wants the same thing in the relationship that she does. They're having sex so they must both be thinking this could turn into something permanent. She assumes that because she's stopped dating other men, he's going to stop dating other women.

Unfortunately, no one let the man in on this little fact.

You can all guess what happens after that. When the woman finds out that her partner has been dating other women, she feels hurt and betrayed. She assumed that he felt the same way she did. The problem is that the couple never actually discussed their relationship. They never sat down and really figured out what each of them wanted and expected from the other.

To a woman, having sex and being exclusive are signs of commitment.

To a man, having sex and being exclusive are nothing more than having sex and being exclusive. And when it comes to men, exclusive simply means, "I'll stay with you until someone better comes along."

There's a communication gap between men and women. Your average man can spend a long time in exclusive mode without ever feeling committed. He has a great woman to share his life with, and he has a regular sex partner. But that doesn't mean he's ready or even considering walking down the aisle with her. The typical woman feels committed much earlier in the relationship than the man does.

They're just not on the same relationship page.

I saw this in action when a couple I knew came over for dinner. They'd been going together for about six months, and I asked the girl, Joanna, how everything was.

"It's terrific!" she said, enthusiastically. "It's nice to be around a guy who isn't afraid of commitment."

I looked over at Bob, Joanna's partner, and I saw a puzzled look on his face. I immediately knew that this was the first time Bob had heard he was in a "committed" relationship. It was clear that Bob hadn't given any thought to the commitment question.

I have a feeling the two of them had a long talk on the way home from the dinner.

Again, though, it's important to understand that men are really looking for commitment. It just takes them longer to get there.

Let's face it; I've met a lot of people who were in relationships that went nowhere. They might have been together for months, if not years, but it seemed like nothing was really taking place in the relationship. They didn't date anyone else and seemed to get along fine, but the relationship never progressed beyond that.

That's because one or both of the partners wasn't committed. And you probably know which one it usually is. In most cases, it's the man. Call it societal pressure, biology, or whatever you want, women just seem to be ready to make the commitment sooner than men. It doesn't mean he won't ever make a commitment to you, it just means it will probably take him longer to decide.

I know these comments are going to strike a nerve with a lot of my female readers. I've heard so many of my female coaching clients say to me, "But he really loves me. We've been going together for eight years, but he's just not ready yet."

"What's he waiting for?" I'll usually ask. "The return of Halley's Comet?"

The truth is that this man is just not committed. He may care for her. I'll even go so far as to admit that he'll probably express his love from time to time. But he's not committed.

You see, until a man is committed to the relationship, not just the woman, he's wearing a parachute. This means that as long as the relationship is flying high and all is right with the world, he's in Heaven. What could go wrong? This is great, for now. Besides, he's got a parachute, right?

He keeps the parachute within reach so he knows that he's covered when things start getting a little rocky. If the plane hits a really bad storm, he can just go and pop the emergency hatch and jump out. If things get difficult in the relationship, he can bail out any time.

Sure, it might be that the plane could weather the storm and he'd never have to jump, but that parachute is his security outlet. He knows that he can just get out of the relationship any time he wants to.

This is difficult to accept for most women. Many of them know it in their guts, though. Deep down, they know that if things got rough, the man would bail out.

If you have a committed relationship, you don't have to worry. You know he'll stick it out when things get rough. He's not going to leave just because the stresses of your job made you cranky or he's disappointed that he got passed over for a raise. You can feel secure even in a room of highly attractive and desirable women. He may look at them and even comment on their beauty, but he won't consider asking one of them out. It just wouldn't cross his mind.

So how can you tell if a man is committed? It's really quite simple. Pay attention to his behavior more than his words, or lack of words. I'm not expecting you to put this book down right now and ask your partner whether he is committed. It probably wouldn't work anyway. He would probably be dumbfounded and would try to change the subject. But there's one sure way to tell. If he's going to be there forever, and if you want to be sure about it, the easiest way is for him to make a public declaration. You will know he's committed when he declares his commitment and devotion in front of friends, family, and the world.

My friend Tom summed it up perfectly for me, when he said, "I loved being with Kathi, and I loved knowing that she was there for me, but in the beginning of the relationship, I wasn't sure if she was going to be the one I was looking for. I still had some doubts and was still thinking there might be someone better suited for me. But, I stayed with her, and there came a time when I realized that she was the one person I wanted to spend the rest of my life with. Once that happened, I couldn't wait to get married to her. The day I stood in front of the entire congregation and professed my love to her is the day that I felt myself connected on a level that was deep and spiritual."

Let me make it perfectly clear, the one sure way to tell if a man is committed is to have a ring and a date. Now, some people out there are going to say, "Marriage is an outdated custom, and it's not needed in today's modern times. We don't need some piece of paper to tell us we're committed." Well, I say they're wrong.

Without that public declaration in front of your family and friends, it's just too easy to walk away when things get rough. He may say he's committed to you, but unless he's said so publicly, he's not committed to maintaining your relationship. He's with you for now, but not necessarily forever. He is not willing to make his feelings public and take himself completely off the dating market.

An oath is a promise or a statement of fact, calling upon something or someone that the person making the oath considers sacred. When you marry, you take an oath to keep your relationship no matter what happens in the future. There's a good reason the traditional wedding vows contain the words that they do. Those words are a public oath that you will remain true to your partner and stay with them for the rest of your life.

Listen, talk is not just cheap -- it's free. If you're with a guy and he tells you that he loves you and is going to spend the rest of his life with you, that's great. But it doesn't mean a lot if he's not willing to make it public and make it permanent.

There's an old saying: "Judge a man by his deeds and not by his words."

This means, forget about what's coming out of the guy's mouth. Instead, watch what the he's doing. That's where the truth really lies. Yes, a public declaration is just a bunch of words. But, the deed or behavior is in the act of declaring in front of witnesses. The specific words are much less important. Watch the behavior, not the words.

Some men feel pressured by their partners to make that commitment. Perhaps the couple has been dating for several years, and she desperately wants to get married. I've even had clients tell me that if their partner doesn't give them a ring by a certain date, they're going to dump him and look for someone else. He, however, feels like Tom in our story above. He loves her and all that, but he's just not sure she's the one he wants to spend the rest of his life with. One the other hand, he doesn't want to lose her because he might not find anyone better. Her friends tell him that she's expecting a ring for Christmas. He's reluctant, but figures he'll get the ring to make her happy. So now they're engaged. She got the commitment she wanted, right? Not necessarily. Remember, there are two parts to the commitment. Part one is the ring. Part two is the date.

Dear Kathy,

I've been with my boyfriend for 4 years. Our relationship is great, but I'm ready to get married and he still keeps putting it off. We went together for 1 year before I moved into his place. After living together for another year he gave me a beautiful diamond ring. I was on cloud nine. I'm sure he's the one and I love him dearly. But after being engaged for two years now, he still won't set a date. He says he wants us to get married, but he just started a new job and wants to make sure that's going to work out first. I don't know what to do. Please help.

Andrea

Dear Andrea,

This is a common problem, especially for young adults. Your boyfriend is just not ready yet, and there's nothing you can do to hurry that along. He is not committed to you. By giving you a ring, he's saying that you're the one for him — at least for now. But he's still not sure you're the one he wants to commit to for the rest of his life. I know it's hard to face that, but it's the truth. Doesn't mean he doesn't love you, he does. Believe him when he says that he's just not ready. The question then becomes, how long are you willing to wait for him? If you try to pressure him into setting a date, he may eventually agree. But it won't make him committed to your relationship. Only he can decide when it's time for him to make that commitment. The decision you need to make becomes how much time do you give him. If you're really eager to get married, consider setting a deadline. But keep it to yourself. If you tell him, he will feel pressured to commit and may agree to marriage just to make you happy. But it still won't make him committed. You deadline may be another 6 months, 1 year, or several years. That's up to you. If he's not ready to commit by that time, you move on. I know it's hard to think about losing him, so you have a tough decision to make.

The question above illustrates part two of the equation. Setting a date. A ring isn't much more than a piece of jewelry if you don't also set a date. This is the true sign that he's committed and ready to make your relationship permanent. It's an important part of the commitment process. Without a date, he still feels he can bail out if someone better comes along. I don't want you to get the idea that all men are afraid of commitment. Remember, they just look at it differently.

And, if you're with a guy who won't stand up and commit to you in a public venue, you might need to reconsider why you're even in that relationship.

Why does it have to be such a big thing, this whole "doing it in public" routine?

Simple.

Public oaths and vows are important.

If you're still thinking that the whole "oath" argument doesn't hold water in today's modern society, think about the following:

- A president is sworn in to office by taking a public oath.
- When you enlist in military service, you take a public oath to obey orders and defend your country.
- When you sign a legal document, it is usually "witnessed" by a third party. The document is also recorded in a public repository for everyone to see.

I'll bet you didn't realize just how prevalent oaths are in today's society.

Ever since there have been weddings, marriage vows have been recited in front of witnesses. These witnesses are an essential part of the ceremony and a legal requirement in most jurisdictions. They provide validation from an outside source as to the enormous undertaking that you have chosen. It doesn't have to the biggest public gathering of the century. It can be just you and a few of your friends. But witnesses are necessary to reinforce the firm commitment you are making to each other.

Think about it this way -- what good are promises made between two people in private? With no one there to take notice of what transpired, it would be impossible to decide, if an argument arises, who said what and how it was said and whether or not the other person heard things correctly.

So, if you're a woman and you're in a relationship, do not automatically assume commitment. It doesn't matter if the man has told you that he loves you. It doesn't matter if he says that he's yours forever. Until he pledges his love to you and takes that public oath that acknowledges his desire to be with you forever, he's just giving you a bunch of words.

When a man makes a public commitment in front of friends and family, he is finally committed to both you and the relationship. Until that moment, however, he is going to be "on the market," and I don't care if he's been in a relationship with a woman for ten years, without ever once cheating on her.

He's still got that parachute on his back.

You'll know when he's ready to make a commitment to you. It's actually pretty simple - - he'll tell you. He'll propose to you, he'll start acting the part of someone who is committed, and before you know it, you'll experience that commitment on a level you didn't even know existed.

On the other hand, do not ask a man to marry you. Just because he says yes, doesn't necessarily make him committed. You may discover years later that he is still not committed. In the back of his mind, he's always going to be thinking, "She's the one who wanted to get married. I wasn't ready." I've had two friends who asked men to marry. They tell me that was the biggest mistake of their lives. If you're going to have a successful relationship, you need to know that the man became committed to you because it was his idea and because he truly wants to spend the rest of his life with you. Here's a good rule for you: the person who commits last is the one who should propose. That person is almost always the man.

I asked Larry, a friend of mine, why it was that he seemed to have a problem with commitment, and I was surprised at his answer.

"I'm not afraid of commitment. I'm afraid of committing ***too soon.*** I mean, I know that I eventually want to settle down with someone, have a family, and grow old together. That's a given. What I hate, though, is that the minute I start to think that I might have found a girl who fits what I'm looking for, she's already thinking of us in terms of being a 'couple.' It tells me that she's already planned everything out, and I just can't handle that."

So, what can you do, then?

- First, understand that just because you have an emotional attachment your partner may not feel the same.

- Second, remember that not dating anyone else means just that. It doesn't mean commitment.

- Third, make sure that you talk about the relationship and how you perceive it. Don't assume that his view of the way things are is the same view as yours. This can avoid a lot of misunderstanding and hurt feelings.

- Fourth, don't put pressure on the relationship to head in a direction that you want it to go. If you try to force your partner to become committed before they're ready, it will not turn out well.

- Lastly, know when it's time to let a relationship go.

If you're looking for commitment, and your partner just flat out isn't looking for the same thing, it might be time to remove him from your list of potential partners and open up a slot for someone else. If you're ready to commit after just a few months, but he needs a few years (or more) you need to ask yourself if you are willing to wait around on the chance that he will eventually commit. Remember, men and women commit on different timetables. If your man's timetable is very different from yours, you may need to find another man. Too many women have wasted years of their lives-years that could have been spent in a loving relationship-waiting for the wrong man to commit.

Don't make the same mistake most women make and assume he's committed to you. Have a conversation about your relationship and where you both think things are headed. Until you are honest with each other about your visions for the future, you can not assume that his are the same as yours.

Chapter Seven

Mistake #6

Dating a Cheater

I f the statistics are to be believed, millions of men and women are cheating in their relationships. Of course, many of them don't even realize or won't admit that they're cheating — and neither do their partners.

When we think of cheating, we tend to think in terms of either marriage or a committed relationship, and sex. If a man is accused of cheating, we're assuming that he's either in a committed relationship or married and is having sex with someone other than his partner. But, that's not necessarily the case.

Cheating doesn't have to be physical. Cheating is the forming of an emotional or physical bond with one person while you are in a relationship with another person.

Think about that for a minute.

"...the forming of an emotional or physical bond..."

In other words, someone can be cheating without ever laying a hand on someone other than their partner. The physical bond we all understand. That's the common definition of cheating. But this emotional bond is something relatively new. One of the things that we've seen with the explosion of the internet is the tremendous number of people who are forming emotional attachments with internet friends. They find themselves in online chat rooms with other people and engage in behavior that can only be described as "cheating."

When you're in the dating phase and you're still shopping for your perfect partner, you have your list of requirements for a mate. As we've discussed in an earlier chapter, your requirements are the traits and characteristics that your partner absolutely must have in order for the relationship to continue and succeed.

If these requirements are not met, the relationship is over. No discussion, that's it. You can have positive requirements, such as the fact that your partner has to be over six feet tall. And, of course, you can have negative requirements – such as the potential partner must not be physically abusive or be an alcoholic or have a drug addiction.

You'd also think that most people would have a requirement that their partner not be a cheater. If you thought that, you thought wrong.

Women, especially, have a problem being firm on the issue of cheating. Oh, sure, most women will say that they won't date a cheater, or that they'll break it off if they find out their partner is cheating, but that's not quite what happens. It's one of the oldest stories out there – a man cheats on his wife or partner, he gets caught, he begs for forgiveness. The woman doesn't want to lose him, so he is forgiven. Some time afterward, the whole thing is replayed and he does it again.

Many women, in fact, will put up with repeat offenders. Putting up with a cheater – even once – means that being faithful is not a requirement for these women.

If you're a woman and you're looking for a good man who will love you, respect you, and treat you the way that you deserve to be treated, it makes sense to list fidelity as a requirement. Probably most women and men would say fidelity is an absolute must for their relationships. However, if you decide that you are, indeed, going to make this a requirement, make sure that you think things through.

If you decide that fidelity is a requirement, you must be prepared to make it a "deal breaker." That means that if your partner cheats, you're gone. No discussing, no arguing, no forgiving. You will end the relationship.

It's scary to think about our partners cheating on us, but pretending that something isn't an issue isn't going to make it go away. No one likes to imagine that the person they're with might cheat on them, especially when it means they will have to end the relationship. But if fidelity is one of your requirements, that's what will happen if you're going to honor our own integrity and be true to yourself.

But, here's some good news — by knowing yourself, by knowing that fidelity is one of your requirements, you will actually be less likely to have to enforce this requirement. If you discuss this matter with your partner and he understands that fidelity is an absolute requirement for you, he will be less likely to cheat.

Plus, if you're ever confronted with an unfaithful partner, it'll be easier to end the relationship. You won't have to worry and ponder and deliberate and vacillate. If you make fidelity a requirement and your partner breaks it, that's it. It's over.

You've spelled out your requirements in advance, and if your partner cheats on you, the end of the relationship falls squarely on their shoulders. Sure, you're going to be sad about it, and you may mourn the end of the relationship, but you'll have absolutely no reason to feel guilty about what happened. After all, they did the cheating, not you. You should never feel guilty for sticking with your convictions.

This is one of the reasons why you need to make sure that your partner understands your requirements – and why you have to stay firm on those requirements. If you're with someone who knows what the rules are, and knows that breaking the rules will have serious consequences, that person is going to be a lot less likely to do anything to jeopardize the relationship.

By setting out your requirements in advance, you are actually practicing "relationship problem prevention."

Jill is a friend that had been in a relationship where she found her partner cheating on her. At the time, he begged for her forgiveness and promised her that it was never going to happen again. Against her better judgment, she decided to give him another chance. After all, they had been together for several years and other than his cheating, the relationship was going well.

"That turned out to be a huge mistake," she admits. "I thought he was going to see how serious I was and stay faithful to me from then on. But the truth is, the moment I took him back, he probably realized that I wasn't the kind of person who he could respect. He knew that I wasn't really serious about his not cheating so I probably wasn't serious about other requirements we had talked about. Looking back on it, I should have walked away from the relationship right then and there. That way, I would have saved myself from further pain down the road. And I would have not wasted more time on a relationship that was doomed."

For most of us, it's difficult to be firm when it comes to someone cheating on us, but the fact is that if we stay strong in our convictions, we will have a lot less pain later on because we're not setting ourselves up for more cheating by our partners.

So you've thought about it and you've decided that fidelity is a requirement for you. Something you need to understand, however, is that even though you might make fidelity an absolute in your relationship when you are first going through the dating process, it might not be that way later on in the relationship.

Before you scream at me, let me explain.

When you're dating, or living together (not recommended), or during the early years of your marriage, you might decide that even one episode of cheating will end the relationship. Now, in the vast majority of cases, that's a very good position to take. Studies have shown that if a partner cheats early in a relationship, they are much more likely to continue cheating.

In other words, if you've been married for only a few years and your husband cheats on you, there's a good chance that he's going to cheat on you again. Even with counseling and interventions, that behavior is usually repeated. Remember we said earlier that people don't change much once they reach adulthood. This is one of those behaviors that usually doesn't change. That doesn't mean that they can't change, it just means that they usually don't. A lot of women don't want to hear that. They want to think that it was an isolated incident and it's never going to happen again. Unfortunately, the facts are working against them, and the sooner these women wake up to the truth, the better off they are going to be.

If it's early in a relationship or early in a marriage and infidelity takes place, the best thing to do is end it. If you're serious about having your partner be faithful to you, now's the time to move on and start over. Rather than subjecting yourself to a cycle of cheating, followed by forgiveness, followed by cheating, followed by forgiveness, you might as well just call it quits. Otherwise, you're just going to be wasting more of your life on someone who isn't going to be true to you.

Ending this relationship will free you to look for a better partner. You can now look for someone who will be faithful to you, someone who will not betray your affections.

What happens if you've been married for many years, however?

Yes, cheating is still cheating. Yes, it's going to hurt you, and yes, it's probably going to damage your relationship forever. There's no getting around that.

But for many of us, the situation is probably different from when we were first dating that person. If you've been married for 20 years, there's a very good chance that you have children. You've also developed a network of shared friends, and you've become a part of your spouse's family. And they've become part of yours. You share a mortgage and you share a history.

You stand to lose a great deal more if you've been married for 20 years, as opposed to if you were newlyweds. And I'm not talking about financially.

Now, don't get me wrong. I'm not saying that if someone cheats, you should stay with them, just because you've built a shared history together. Nothing could be further from the truth. I am definitely not recommending that you forgive a cheater, simply because the two of you have logged in a lot of years together. That's going to be your decision. The point that I'm trying to get across is that you should take a look at the whole situation. Something that is a requirement early on in your relationship may not be after many years together.

Another thing to consider is this. If you've been married for 20 years and your spouse cheats, it's more likely to be an isolated incident. Many people start wondering what life's all about as they get older. They have the infamous 'mid-life crisis' and start to wonder if they're still attractive to the opposite sex. At this point, many men and women are tempted to have an affair. When this happens, it's usually a one time thing. While it's still very painful and hurtful to the relationship, these are the types of affairs that can sometimes be forgiven. It's not really a pattern of behavior for the partner, just a desire to recapture their youth. This is another reason why cheating after many years together may not immediately end the relationship.

So far, we've actually been concentrating on physical infidelity. This is where one partner has sex outside the relationship. But as we mentioned earlier, there's another kind of cheating and some people consider it even worse than physical infidelity.

I'm talking about emotional cheating.

This is where one partner develops an emotional connection with someone at work, someone they've met socially or maybe even someone they've met on the internet. Your partner might never actually meet this other person face to face, but they are still cheating. All of the thoughts and emotions that they are giving the other person are thoughts and emotions they should be sharing with you.

Dear Kathy,

I'm not sure if I have a problem or not. I never thought that Eddie (my boyfriend of 3 years) would cheat on me. He says that he isn't, but I think he is. When I was on our computer sending an email, he received an instant message from a girl. From the tone of the message, it was obvious that the two of them had some kind of relationship going on. So I decided to go and check his emails. I was shocked to find out that there were emails from this girl going back ten months, and when I looked at some of the emails Eddie had sent to her, I couldn't believe it. Apparently they have never even met, but he shared things with this girl that he'd never shared with me. I can't even begin to tell you how hurt I felt when I read those emails. I confronted Eddie and he blew up. He said I had no right to read his emails and we got into a huge argument. He say's he's not cheating because there's nothing physical going on. What do you say?

Laura

Dear Laura,

  Just because Eddie has not met this girl in person does not make him innocent. He is definitely cheating. Although it's not physical, the emotional attachment he's formed with this girl is just a real as if they'd been dating. This is obvious because he's apparently shared some very deep and private thoughts with her. His reaction to your confrontation is typical of cheaters. They get angry with you for finding them out, and usually try to make it your fault. Whether you want to continue this relationship or not is a question you'll have to answer. If you do want to try to stay with Eddie, he must immediately give up all contact with this girl. That means no phone calls, no emails, no instant messenger, no nothing. He doesn't get to email her and say goodbye; it stops. How will you know if he's keeping his word not to contact her? He must give you access to his cell phone and email account so you can check from time to time. I know this sounds like an invasion of privacy, but remember he's the one who cheated. You have nothing to feel guilty about. If he's not willing to let you check his phone and email occasionally, he's not serious about continuing your relationship. If he's willing to comply, you still may not want to stay, but that decision is up to you.

You see, whether the cheating is emotional or physical, infidelity comes into the picture when one partner is sharing his or her personal and intimate life with a third person outside the relationship. Whether it's physical or not, the fact that a partner has been having a relationship with someone else is devastating. While most people are understandably hurt when it comes to physical infidelity, it seems that they are less likely to forgive the emotional infidelity than the physical infidelity. This is especially true of women.

Christina is a woman who caught her husband cheating on her with a girl he met when he was on a business trip. Instead of ending the marriage, she decided to forgive him. She did, however, make one thing very clear to him:

"I told him that I was willing to overlook the mistake he made. He was on a business trip, he was probably drinking, and things probably got out of hand. I could live with that. But, if I'd found out that he was having an affair and sharing all of our intimate details with someone else, that would be the end of the marriage. I'd have him out on the street so fast that he wouldn't be able to think straight. A one night stand I can understand. I don't like it, but I understand. But an emotional attachment to another woman is too much. I won't put up with that."

So, when it comes to issues of infidelity, you need to decide just what it is you're going to tolerate. Are you going to accept a man who sleeps with another woman? Are you going to be able to be with a girl who spends time in online chat rooms, flirting with other people?

I'm not going to make that decision for you. It comes down to individual preference and where the line is going to be drawn by you in your relationships.

Why do some women tolerate infidelity by suffering through repeated episodes of unfaithfulness? For most of us, it's inconceivable to imagine that someone could go through something over and over and over again, but these women are living proof that not everyone is like us.

In most cases, the man promises that he'll never do it again. He tells her that he's sorry. Now, at this point, he probably is. He may even cry and beg for her forgiveness. And he's really sincere when he says that he'll be faithful from then on. He wants to be faithful and he probably even loves her. But, that doesn't mean that he won't do it again. He probably will.

So, why would a woman stay with a man like that? There are any number of reasons, and we can't even begin to guess at what goes on in someone else's mind. From what some women have said, however, it seems that these women are usually afraid of being alone. Remember our previous chapter on needing to have a relationship? When you need to have a man, any man, you will put up with behaviors that you otherwise wouldn't. Infidelity is one of them. When you are afraid of being alone, you can rationalize that he'll change, he'll be true. Otherwise you'd have to end the relationship and start over again. You may think that being with a cheater is better than not being with anyone at all. I don't believe that. Being alone is better than being with someone untrustworthy and disrespectful.

As incredible as it sounds, there are other women who stay with a cheater because they think that they are, somehow, the cause of the cheating. I've had women tell me that they must have done something wrong to make their husbands stray. It must be their fault somehow. Then, they ask me what they can do to make it up to their husbands!

Think about that — the man cheats, and the woman is feeling sorry and guilty over what he did! This was illustrated in the question above. Eddie tried to make Laura feel guilty for finding out that he was cheating. It's amazing how many women fall for this trick. Then they get so caught up in feeling guilty that they forget it was the man who betrayed them.

There's another side of this we haven't discussed yet. What if you're the one dating a man already married or in a relationship? You might tell yourself that you're not doing anything wrong. Unfortunately, when you take a step back and look at things realistically, you're dating a cheater. You might think he's cheating on his wife, but he's cheating on you as well. Either way, he's a cheater.

What does that say about you? What does it say about your choice of men?

Some of you might be currently dating a married man. You tell yourself that "we really love each other." When someone points out the fact that the man is cheating on his wife, you're quick to say that it's not like that. He's in a bad marriage. His wife doesn't love him. His wife doesn't understand him. This is common talk from a cheater. You need to wake up and face the reality of the situation.

You're dating a man who doesn't have the guts or the integrity to leave a bad marriage. When things in his relationship don't go the way he wants, what does he do? Rather than try to make it work or leave, he hooks up with another woman. That other woman is you.

If you really look at what his behavior is saying, not what his words are, he's telling you that his marriage really isn't as bad as he makes it sound. Oh, sure, he might have told you a terrific tale about how mistreated he is at home, and how his wife doesn't know anything about him, and how she just doesn't have time for him or seem to care about him. He tells you that the love has gone from his marriage and he's living a dry and dull lie with his wife.

Then, you came along, and everything changed. You've given him a reason to have hope again. You're in his thoughts all the time and you're the answer to a prayer. Meeting you was the best thing that ever happened, and he's going to work on finding a way for you and him to be together forever.

If you believe that, you're deluding yourself. He's lying to you, and on some level, I'm sure you know that. No matter how you slice it, no matter what angle you come at it from, you have to face the reality of the situation.

You're involved with a cheater. He's cheating with you, though. So, it's not like he's cheating on you, right? Wrong. When he's with his wife, he's cheating on you. It amazes me how women can rationalize all kinds of reasons why it's okay to stay with a married man. And these are otherwise normal, sane, rational women.

You might think that it's an old cliché, but the fact is that most married men talk a good game. They're really good at it because they've usually had a lot of practice. They are providing you with talk. There's never going to be any follow through. Oh, sure, they'll tell you that they're "going to leave their wives, someday." But someday never comes. The time is never right, there's always an excuse but it will be soon.

Dear Kathy,

I've been with a married man for 10 ½ years. He's been separated for 11 years but refuses to get a divorce. I'm not looking for marriage from him but I don't like him staying married to someone else. I left him once and came back to a bunch of promises.

It's been 2 years and nothing has changed. I'm contemplating moving out on my own but I'm afraid of being alone and I will miss him a lot. I have this overwhelming feeling to live alone once in my life, but I'm so afraid. Am I wasting my time with this man? He is 18 years older than me and I'm sure I can find someone else but I feel guilty.

Sharon

Dear Sharon,

You've been seeing a married man for over 10 years and you ask if you're wasting your time? Surely you know the answer to that yourself. It doesn't take much to see that if he wanted to finalize his divorce, he would have by now. But he has a great excuse not to commit to your relationship because he's still legally married. As you've already seen, he may promise you things but he's not going to change. Many women, just like you, stay with unavailable men because they are afraid of being alone. Of course you will miss him, but you will get over him. You've already spent 10 years with someone who will never be committed to you. How much more time do you need to waste before you decide to make a change?

The sooner you move out, the sooner you can move on. You need to have the courage to leave and get on with your life. Start today to look for someone who is more available and wants the same kind of relationship you do.

Sharon is a typical example of women who date married men. And she was even living with her married man. She threatened to leave and he promised whatever she wanted, but nothing changed after that. So she continued to do what most women do. She decided to wait. She has taken herself off the dating market. She has made herself unavailable to eligible single men, and she continues to wait.

Consider the married men who still live with their wives and have a woman on the side. They have made promises to both women. So both are waiting, both are off the dating market, and both believe his deceit. Meanwhile, he is having it both ways – he's got his marriage, and he's got his girlfriend.

But, let's say that you find the guy who actually decides that he is going to leave his wife. That's right. You've found the atypical married man who follows through, and he moves out. He moves in with you, and something incredible happens – you discover that you really don't like him. Oh, sure, when he wasn't with you all the time, it was easy to overlook the flaws that are now glaringly obvious. Or, in another scenario, he moves out from his home and he comes to the realization that he misses his family. And now that you've become his steady girlfriend, you are no longer as exciting as you once were. The thrill of doing something he shouldn't be doing is gone. He decides that he wants to be with his wife.

There's more bad news. Research shows that when men leave their wives, they usually do not marry the woman they left home for. Yes, they might remarry eventually, but it won't be to the woman they left their families for. So if you're the 'other woman' it won't be you that he marries. If he leaves his wife and home and eventually remarries, it will be to someone else, not you.

Are you beginning to see why trying to have a relationship with a cheater just isn't a good idea?

"When I started seeing Sam," a friend of mine told me, "he was married. He told me that his wife was a real shrew. The way that he described her, she was a horrible woman who only married him for his money, and there was no love in their relationship. He was looking for someone that he could really open himself up to", he told me, "and I found myself falling in love with him."

"Naturally, everyone told me that I was being very stupid. They told me that he wasn't going to ever leave his wife, but I was sure they were wrong. I was sure that what he and I had was special. We kept this up for three years, and then, one night, he told me that he still loved his wife and he wanted to really give his marriage a chance."

"I was devastated. I couldn't believe that I'd wasted three years of my life on a man who I now realized had no intention of ever being with me for the rest of our lives."

I'm not making any judgments about how you should live your life. I'm just telling you what I've learned through the years, and what I've seen happen. Married men who cheat usually go from one girlfriend to another and have no intention of ever leaving their wives. They're just habitual cheaters.

If that's the kind of relationship you want for yourself, that's your choice. But most of us want more. We want someone who will be committed to us and our relationship. We don't want to be second on our man's relationship list. When you're shopping for new furniture you wouldn't look at a piece that already had a sold tag on it. Why would you do that when you're looking for someone to spend your life with? When you're shopping for the man who will become your life partner, don't waste your time with someone who's already taken.

Chapter Eight

Mistake # 7

Thinking He Will Change

Many women think they're out to find their ideal mate; that they are looking for someone special to share their life with. Nothing could be further from the truth. They enter a new relationship with someone even though that person clearly doesn't fit their relationship requirements. If they were actually holding out for their perfect partner, they wouldn't enter into relationships with men who are so obviously wrong for them.

Why would a woman willingly enter a relationship with someone who isn't right for her? The answer to that one is easy. She thinks that she can change him.

When you're out shopping for shoes, would you buy a pair that's the wrong color? You could always have them dyed to change them to the color you want. You wouldn't buy a pair that's too big and try to stuff tissue paper in the toes to make them fit. And you certainly wouldn't buy a pair of flats if you want heels and try to add your own heels to them. If they are not what you're looking for, you move on to the next store and keep looking. After all, there are lots of different colors, sizes, and styles out there to choose from You wouldn't even think twice about going to another store, or several stores until you found what you wanted. The same should be true when we're looking for a partner. Especially if you're looking to spend the rest of your life with, isn't it worth taking the time to find the right one?

But many women find a man and try to make him fit what they want. Not only is that a lot of trouble to go through, there's no guarantee he will change. Wouldn't it be better if you were just to hold off until you found what you were really looking for?

What typically happens is that when someone isn't in a relationship, they start to panic. They wonder if they're ever going to find someone. That little relationship clock starts to tick in their head and they get worried that they'll never be able to find someone. They want someone they can spend the rest of their life with so they better get on it. They need someone right now! So the next person they start to date becomes the one.

Sure, he might not be everything they're looking for, but with a little work, they can probably make this person become what they want. If he'd just change a few little things, he'd be acceptable. Notice I said acceptable, not perfect or not necessarily even desirable.

If you go into a relationship with that kind of thinking, you'll be in for a rude awakening. No matter what you might have heard, no matter what you might have read, and no matter what your family and friends tell you, the odds are stacked against you if you think you can take someone who isn't right for you and change them until they're the person that you're looking for.

I know I've said this before, but it's worth repeating because it's so hard for women to accept. People do not change much through life — and if they do change, it's because they choose to change. No one can really change another person. Most experts agree that a person's personality is pretty much set in place by the time that they are twenty to twenty-five years of age. It doesn't mean they can't change after that, it only means that you can not make them change. They will only change if they decide they want to.

People are individuals. Everyone has his own needs, his own desires, his own goals, his own fears. It's nearly impossible for outside forces to act upon a person and make them change. In some cases, there is scientific evidence that certain personality traits seem to be "hard wired" into a person. This means that certain personality traits can be just as much a part of them as their height or their hair color. Keep in mind that we're not talking about total personality, however, only certain traits.

Again, this is not to say that no one ever changes. People can change. However, before they change, they must want to change. It has to come from something inside of them, and not from external pressure. I want to make sure you understand the difference here. Just as you can change some things about yourself if you want to, others can too. But you will not change that something just because someone else asked you to. If it's something you do not want to change, you will not do it. The same is true for others. They have to want to make a change or it's not going to happen. Oh, there might be a change for a time, but it's not going to be a permanent one.

A common example here involves weight. Many people are overweight. They know they are and they are not really happy with the way they look. However, all the nagging in the world will not get you to lose weight if you are one of those people. Even if the nagging is from someone you love dearly, it still won't be enough to get you to diet. It only makes you start to resent the other person. Yes, you could lose weight but you will not do it for someone else. If and/or when you decide it's important to you to lose weight, you will do it, not before.

Dear Kathy,

I've been married 3 years to Sam. He drinks a lot and it's really starting to bother me. When we first started dating I knew he drank a lot. He'd go out with his friends 3-4 nights a week and get drunk. But he always went to work on time so I thought it was no big deal. That was okay when we were young, but I think it's time for him to grow up and be more responsible. He still gets drunk several nights a week and we argue about it a lot. I've asked him to stop drinking during the week and explained how I feel about it. He promised to cut back and he did for a few months. Now he's back to the same old thing. Last night we had a huge fight and I told him that if he didn't stop drinking I was leaving. I don't want to leave because I really love him. I just want him to change. How do I get him to stop drinking so much?

Jill

Dear Jill,

As you're finding out, you can not make someone change. Sam could cut back on his drinking if he wants to, but so far he hasn't wanted to enough. So the answer to your question is you can't get him to stop drinking so much. What you can do, and what you must do, is decide if you're going to accept it or not. If you decide to accept it, you have to stop complaining about it all the time. Accepting his drinking means you will not nag him about it and you will keep silent on that issue. If you decide that you can't accept it your only option is to leave. I know it's difficult to face, but this is the reality. It's clear that this is an important issue for you and I think you'll have a hard time accepting his drinking even if you try. But since you're already married, it's worth a try. Maybe the two of you can agree on some compromise where he can have 1 or 2 beers a night during the week and drink more on weekends if he wants. Think about what you might be able to compromise on and have a serious talk with Sam about it. If he's not willing to compromise, it's time to move on.

Jill's problem shows what happens when we try to change someone else. There's a lot of fighting about it and finally the other person agrees to change. They may even do it. But if they're doing it for you the change will not be permanent. Sooner or later, and usually not too much later, they will be back to their previous behavior. That's because they didn't do it for themselves, they did it for someone else. Since they didn't really think there was a problem to begin with, they're not going to stick with the change.

One client named Lauren was dating a guy, I'll call him Rick. At first, things were going really well, but then, Lauren started to notice that Rick was a little on the "immature" side. He had a kind of crude sense of humor, at times, and he didn't seem to take a whole lot of things seriously. But, Lauren chose to ignore the warning signs that were showing up, and she told herself that she would be able to help Rick "grow up." He would change as they got older and their relationship matured. It didn't work out that way, she admits.

"At first, I could tell that he was really trying," Lauren explains, "but it seemed like for every step forward we made, he would just backslide and we'd be right back to the same place as where we started. Eventually, I came to the realization that he wasn't going to be the kind of man I needed in my life. I wanted someone a little more serious, a little more grown up. But I'd already put six months into an exclusive relationship with him so I didn't want to just give up. I tried to get him to change for another three months before I finally realized it just wasn't going to work."

That's where the problem comes in. Too many women are out there, spending time and energy trying to make a man "fit" into their requirements, but what they should be doing is crossing those men off their lists and moving on. They should stop wasting their time trying to change someone who's not right for them and spend their time finding someone else who is more suited to them.

Another area where women try to change men is in the area of marriage. Many men will go into a relationship and be totally up front about what they're looking for. They don't want to lead women on when they're not looking for marriage. But, the woman is determined to be in a relationship, so she decides that she's going to put that whole "no marriage" issue to the side. She can look at it later, once they're a couple, and then, she can work on getting him to come around to her way of thinking. She thinks that once he falls in love with her, he'll want to get married just as much as she does.

One of my male clients tells me this story. He's divorced and is really not interested at this point in marrying again. He will someday, but not anytime soon. But he enjoys dating and his friends are constantly fixing him up with available women. He always tells these women when they first start dating that he's not looking for a serious relationship so they have the chance to stop seeing him now if they're looking for a commitment. But they usually keep dating him. A few months to by and the woman is now wanting an exclusive relationship. You can guess how this turns out. When he reminds her that's not what he wants, the woman gets mad and usually won't see him again. He ends up with the bad reputation because he's dated many women and has yet to settle down.

By the way, isn't it interesting that most women are assuming that it's the man's job to change? They look at a man who isn't right for them, and rather than saying, "If I'm going to be with him, either I'm going to have to change. This just won't work the way I am." They wind up saying, "If I'm going to be with him, I'm going to have to find a way to make him change."

Naturally, when the relationship is first starting, the woman doesn't mention this to the man. She doesn't want to cause problems so early in the relationship so she decides not to speak up. So the poor guy is thinking that she's fine with who he is, thinking that he's finally met someone who "gets" him Then just when he starts to let his guard down and starts to finally relax, the woman starts in on her "Project: Rebuild" assignment. The poor guy never even knows what hit him.

As we said earlier, most experts will tell you that a woman has very little chance of changing her partner's worst habits. Sure, there are always some people who do change. But for the most part, what you see at the beginning of the relationship is what you get. If more women accepted that and decided to move on earlier in the relationship, there would be a lot less turmoil down the road.

This doesn't just go for women, either. There are men out there who try to change the women in their lives. For example, one young man was attracted to a bright, funny, charming girl who is really outgoing and exuberant. Those were the qualities that drew him to her. However, once they started dating, he preferred her to be "less out there" and not to be so outgoing, especially around other men. He wanted her to stop being herself. Needless to say, the relationship didn't last for very long.

If you take a look at some of the strongest and most enduring relationships, you'll see that they are built on a foundation of mutual respect and acceptance. This is an incredibly important concept to grasp. The relationships that truly last are the ones where you don't have two people who are trying to change each other, but who have enough in common so that they can work through their differences.

In fact, we can go a step further than that. Some of the relationships that last the longest are ones where there are differences between the man and the woman, and those differences are celebrated.

One of the worst things that ever happened to society was the notion of the whole "Soulmate" myth. A lot of people think that we all have a soulmate out there — someone who is our mirror image...who likes what we like, who hates what we hate. Someone who is just like us.

The reality, though, is that many of us don't like the qualities in ourselves that we see in others. Let's say that you're a very talkative person who likes to dominate a conversation. Do you think that you're going to be happy in a relationship with someone who does the same thing? If you both like to talk a lot and dominate the conversation, you're not going to get along. Odds are that you'll find yourself disliking the person more and more. This is how we came to the conclusion that opposites attract. If you are very talkative, you'll probably get along better with someone who is more reserved, someone who is perfectly happy listening to you talk for hours.

Sure, you need to have certain things in common. If you're a vegetarian, you're probably not going to be that happy with someone who goes hunting. By the same token, if you're someone who is very religious and spiritual, you're not going to be happy with an atheist or an agnostic. You may not require someone who is the same religion as you, but he must be a believer.

There needs to be a common foundation, but it doesn't have to be identical. In most cases, if you have 80 to 90 percent of things in common, you're probably doing really well, and you don't have anything to worry about. This takes us back to our list of relationship requirements; the must haves and the nice to haves.

Some people just don't understand what's wrong with trying to change someone. Trisha, a friend of mine, met a guy that she really liked. Within a month, she was trying to change him.

"Eric was a great guy," she said, "but there were a couple of little things about him that I wanted to change. At first, I tried to get him to change without being obvious about it, but then, I just had to come right out and tell him what I was looking for. He got very upset. It took me a while to realize that I had, in a way, told him that there was something wrong with him, and if he just did these couple of things for me, he'd be 'fixed.' Even though he tried to make the changes so that I'd be happy, they didn't work.

We eventually had to break up, because neither one of us was happy in the relationship."

Now, if Trisha had gone into the relationship with her eyes open, she could have seen these that "couple of little things" were obviously bigger than she thought — especially if they led to the relationship breaking up. If she'd been honest with herself (and with Eric) from the beginning, she could have saved the two of them a lot of heartache.

Most of us don't go into a relationship with the intention of changing anyone. We engage in something that I'll call "magical thinking" — where we enter a relationship and just assume that the other person is somehow going to "magically" change himself. We won't have to ask him to change. He'll just gradually become the perfect person we want him to be. That's not a good way to go into a relationship.

The strange thing is that a lot of women don't realize what they're doing. They just think that once the man is in a relationship with them, he's going to change. If you try to pin them down on why they think this is going to happen, you'll see that they actually don't know. It's just going to happen. The fact is — it isn't.

Let's look at this from the man's point of view. You're now the man in this relationship. You're yourself when you enter the relationship, and you think that the girl likes you for who you are. Everything is going along just great, then all of a sudden she's telling you what she wants you to do in order to change. You didn't even know there was a problem. This seems to come out of left field, and before you know it, you're having arguments and the relationship is in trouble.

There's also another subtle way that women try to change men, even if they're not aware of it. It has to do with their list of requirements. They have this "dream man" in their head, their prince charming. They seem to think that men are made out of clay and can be molded into this ideal that's in their subconscious. For some women, they aren't even aware that's what they're doing.

"When I first started seeing Kevin," says Doreen, a computer programmer from San Diego, "I saw so much potential in him. I just knew that if I could work with him, I could get him to see what I saw in him. Then everything would work out. At the time, I don't even think that I was aware of what I was doing. All I know is that once we started to seriously get involved, I found myself doing more and more things to try to get him to change. This led him to get really upset with me, and I can't say that I blame him. I sort of blindsided him with what I was doing."

Women need to look at that list before the relationship really kicks into high gear, and they need to seriously think about it. If there are things on that list that they simply "must have" and the man doesn't have those qualities, they need to end it quickly and permanently. It's not fair to either of them to think she can change him. Just because they are in a relationship doesn't mean he's going to want to change.

One of the traps that a woman can fall into is thinking that each next step of the relationship is going to get the man to change.

"When we're dating, he'll change…"

"When we're serious about each other, he'll change…"

"When we're engaged, he'll change…"

"When we're married, he'll change…"

The truth is that he's probably not ever going to change. We've all had friends who married someone knowing he wasn't right. But they just knew he'd change once they were married. That's not fair to the man, and not fair to you. The sooner the truth comes out about the relationship; the sooner both of you can move on and find the right person. Move on and find someone closer to what you're looking for.

Lastly, however, there are those women who enter a relationship and think that they can

change a man, only to find out that they can't.
Then they try to change themselves.

A woman gets involved with a man who goes
out and parties with his friends a lot. The
woman tells herself that she can eventually get
him to change, once she's really able to "work
with him." She puts on those blinders and
charges ahead into the relationship. You all
know by now what happens. He doesn't change.

Frankly, why should he? This is who he is, and
this is who he's always been. When they started
dating she knew who he was. So why in the
world would he want to change?

Naturally, this leaves the woman in a bind.
After all, she's involved with a man that won't
change for her, and that's causing a strain in the
relationship. Since the relationship can't
continue as it is, the only alternative is for her to
change. If he won't change, she will. After all,
they love each other and she really wants this to
work out. This is a very bad idea and still will
not work.

Remember what we talked about earlier, when it
came to change? You can't make someone else
change unless that person sincerely wants to
change. Well, that same principle holds true for
those people who think that they can change
who they are so that they can stay in a
relationship.

"I was dating a guy," Laura, a cashier from Des Moines, Iowa explained, "and I thought that I was really in love with him. He was cool, and really good looking, and there were girls all over him. This was really a turn-on because he was so hot, and yet, he was dating me. But, once we started to date exclusively, I started to get jealous, and I asked him to stop flirting with other girls. He told me that he wasn't flirting with them —that was just who he was. I didn't push it, because I didn't want to ruin things between us, so I thought that I could just learn to deal with it."

"At first, I did a pretty good job. Yeah, it bothered me to see some cute blonde come over and lean close to him, but I told myself that he didn't want a jealous girlfriend. So I kept my cool, at least on the outside. On the inside, though, it was tearing me up. I'd come back from a date and I'd want to rip out my hair from all the tension that was building up inside of me."

"Finally, things came to a head because I couldn't keep it in any longer. We went out, and he was just being his usual self, but that was the night that everything came exploding out. I yelled at him and told him what a bad boyfriend he was. I cried and made a complete spectacle of myself. Later that night, I realized that he hadn't really done anything wrong. I just couldn't change who I was and I couldn't overlook the way he was around other women. So I ended the relationship, and I wound up with a guy who truly wouldn't ever look at another woman."

Women need to understand that if they are with a man who isn't right for them, the smart thing to do is end things immediately. Don't bother playing around and trying to be someone who you aren't. You might succeed for a little while, but sooner or later, things are going to reach the boiling point and you're not going to be able to hold it in any longer. You must be true to yourself and not try to be someone else. The same is true for the man you're dating. Have enough respect for him that you won't ask him to be someone he's not. If you really love and respect him, you'll accept him the way he is. If that's not the right person for you, keep looking.

It's better to end things before they get too serious rather than to continue down the road. Once you have two kids, a mortgage, and a crummy marriage is no time to realize you just aren't compatible. A little pain in the short run is better than a lot of pain in the long run. The longer you stick with a doomed relationship and try to make it work, the more painful it will be when you finally break up.

If you can avoid this common mistake, you will save yourself a lot of heartache. We've all been in relationships with the wrong person. The more time you have invested in the relationship, the harder you will try to make it work whether that means trying to get your partner to change or trying to change yourself. You can learn to recognize early on when someone is not right for you. Rather than trying to make those shoes fit, keep shopping till you find the ones you're looking for. Keep looking for those ruby slippers.

Chapter Nine

Mistake #8

Thinking Families Don't Matter

Does it sometimes seem as if people don't get along as well as they once did? You can blame technology for that.

With the modern world we live in, there's absolutely no need for any of us to get along with the "real" world. We don't even have to leave our house if we don't want to. We can work from home, order dinner from home, have everything we need delivered do our front door. We can create our own private, personalized world. In many homes throughout the country, there are more television sets than there are people in the house. A friend of mine is proud to have a television in every room of his house -- including all three bathrooms, as well as a television built into the side of his refrigerator.

"It's great," he tells me. "I can completely submerge myself in football and never miss a minute of the game no matter what else I'm doing. I can leave the world at the door."

Some of you might not think that's a big deal, but are you aware of how much something like that has changed the family dynamic? Growing up, I remember watching television with my family. At night, I'd sit there with my mom and dad, and we'd be together, watching whatever programs were on. With only one television in the house, we all sat together and watched the same thing. Years have gone past, and I couldn't tell you more than a handful of the shows that we watched. But I can tell you how great it felt to be with my family every night.

Nowadays, families don't even watch television together. Everyone goes to a different room to watch whatever it is they want to watch. In some cases, they'll have the same program on in different rooms. Everyone wants to be in charge of the remote and be able to choose what he wants to watch when he wants to watch it. People want to be by themselves and they want to be in charge.

Let's face it, though -- we can't just lay the blame at the feet of television. Ever hear about something called an iPod? Almost everyone has a personal mp3 player. Just put your earbuds in, turn on the music, and tune out the world.

Let's go further.

There was a time when you bought a cassette or a compact disc -- and you bought the entire album. There were two or three songs that you really liked, and half a dozen that you weren't crazy about. Well those days are gone. Now, you can buy only the songs that you want. You might as well forget about disc jockeys with their playlists on the radio. Thanks to satellite and internet radio, those are being phased out. Now there are all kinds of "personalized" music options available to us.

But wait, it gets better.

You're driving down the highway, and you glance over at the minivan next to you. There's Dad behind the wheel, concentrating on traffic. Next to him, Mom is sitting with her iPod headphones on, tuning into her own little world. In the back, the cute little girl watches DVDs from a portable player, and the little boy has his Nintendo DS Lite to occupy him. With all the constant input, is it any wonder that talking is becoming a thing of the past?

Don't get me wrong. I think technology can be a wonderful thing. Writing this book is so much easier on a computer than doing it by hand. In fact, I never would have finished if I had to write every word out longhand. Just to think about all the writing and rewriting is overwhelming. I know that using computers and today's modern appliances is an immense improvement over the way the world once was. But, there are also times when technology can have a negative impact on us.

It helps to feed this whole notion of "me." We're living in a world where it's all about "me." We want what we want, when we want it. We don't want to wait. We can download songs that we want instantly, we can get the movies that we want to see beamed directly to our homes, and we can prepare a dinner in our microwave in under five minutes.

That doesn't mean that it's always a good thing, though. (especially the microwave dinners!) Too often, we become so wrapped up in our own feelings that we don't even take anyone else's feelings into consideration. This whole "It's all about me" attitude is hurting us in many aspects of our lives. We are all so busy doing our own thing that we're not noticing the people who are around us. And why should we? They're all too busy doing their own thing to notice that we don't notice them.

Part of the blame can be laid at the feet of parents. We all want to do the best we can for our children, and the thought that we might do anything that could cause the kids to dislike us makes us feel uneasy. There are times, however, when a parent simply has to be a parent --

regardless of how that is going to make the child feel. When a parent makes a child go to bed at a reasonable hour or keeps that child from eating too much junk food and becoming obese, they are doing two things -- the first thing is they are acting like responsible parents.

The second thing is they are teaching their children that it's not always about them. There are consequences to what happens when we find ourselves totally self-centered. Once we start to think that the only opinions that matter are ours, we find ourselves heading down a very slippery slope. When we stop taking into account the way that other people think about us, we sometimes wind up making some serious mistakes. There are times when we have to consider what other people think.

My friend Vivian learned this lesson the hard way. She met a man while she was working in Boulder, and she started up a relationship with him. Some of her friends tried to tell her that he didn't seem to be the right man for her, but Vivian didn't want to hear that. She thought she knew what was best for her.

"I thought I knew him better than they did," she admits, "and whenever they pointed out some of his flaws, I just refused to accept what they were saying. I kept on telling myself that it didn't matter what they thought. The only thing that mattered was how I thought -- and I thought that I loved him. How could they know what was better for me than I did myself? Unfortunately, it didn't turn out the way I thought. And in the end, I sort of just wound up making a fool of myself. They turned out to be right. I was blinded by my desire to have a steady boyfriend. Looking back on it, I could have saved myself a lot of trouble and a lot of pain if I'd just listened to what my friends were trying to tell me from the beginning."

Of course, Vivian is not alone. Many of us have fallen into the same trap. We've gotten into relationships that our families and friends don't approve of. Since we are adult, independent women, we can make our own decisions. Quite a few men and women wind up getting engaged before ever introducing their prospective spouse to their family. Once the date's been set, they'll go to their friends and family and make the announcement. Then, since it's a "done deal," there's no need to seek the advice of our families. They may introduce their fiancée to the family, but they don't want their opinions.

I know there are those who are going to complain that it's not important to have the approval of our family and friends. After all, we're living in modern times, right? This isn't the turn-of-the-previous century where arranged marriages took place, and where families could prohibit a marriage by not giving their blessing to the union. In today's brave new world, we're able to make our own decisions, and we don't need input or approval from anyone. Yeah -- and, in the words of Dr. Phil, "How's that working out for you?"

So, for the sake of argument, let's say that you're considering getting input from friends and family. Notice, by the way, that I said "input." I didn't say "approval." If you're out shopping for a new dress, don't you usually take a friend with you? You want some input from them about the color, style, and fit. If a friend can't go with you to help pick it out, you will come home and try it on for them. You definitely want another opinion before you cut the tags off and it's yours forever. This doesn't mean you will blindly do whatever they say. But you will listen to their opinion and consider it before making your final decision. Shouldn't you do this with your relationship as well? Ask for input from your family and friends. You may not blindly break it off if they don't immediately love your date, but you'll consider what they have to say. After all, it's one thing to keep an open mind and hear what those who care about you have to say -- but it's something else entirely to just do whatever it is that they say.

What are the advantages to having that input? Why is it so important for your partner to meet your family and friends? The answer is simple:

They can see things more clearly.

When we get into relationships and we're in the infatuation phase, we don't have the greatest eyesight in the world. We just don't see clearly when it comes to the person we're involved with. Oh, we might tell ourselves that we know him better than anyone else, but believe it or not, we often fail to see the person for who they are. You've heard the old saying "Love is Blind." When you're in a developing relationship with someone it's hard to be objective about them and see them clearly.

This is really evident when sex comes into the picture. If we're having sex with someone, it's less likely that we're going to want to hear the truth about him or her. After all, if that person isn't measuring up to the standards of our friends and our families, that must mean there's something wrong with us for sleeping with them, right? So if you're having sex with the person, you really need to take a step back and keep an open mind as to what others around you might be saying.

Plus, when we're in a romantic relationship, we tend to overlook certain character defects or flaws. This is caused by the whole notion of "romance." For some reason, we tend to overlook the little flaws individuals have. We only think about the romance and how good we feel when we're with them. Would you keep a dress that had a hole in it just because the rest of it looked really good on you? I don't think so.

Even though the dress is mostly perfect, you couldn't overlook that one little flaw.

Another reason why it's important to meet the family is that your partner is going to behave differently with your family and friends. He needs your acceptance to continue the relationship, but he may be more of himself with them. In other words, they might see the "real" him better than you can. He doesn't necessarily need their approval so he can let his guard down a little.

When you first have your family and friends meet him, make sure that you take yourself out of the picture long enough for them to get to know him. It's okay to leave him alone with them. Again, if you're there, he might be behaving the way you want him to. This is not what you want. You want those who care about you and know you well to see him for who he is. Then they will be more likely to see if he's a good match for you.

Remember, the more eyes you have on him, the more likely it is that you'll get a complete picture as to who he is. That doesn't mean line up all the relatives for him to meet like a police line-up. He doesn't have to meet them all at one time. But he should meet those closest to you; the ones who will always be part of your life. This doesn't just apply to your family, of course.

You need to see how he interacts with his family as well.

You would be amazed at the number of adult men out there who have not grown up. Sure, they might have their own apartments and they might hold down steady jobs, but when it comes to emotional maturity, they're seriously lacking. These men are the ones who are "Peter Pans" -- and they're looking for Wendy to come along and take care of them.

What is his relationship with his mother? When it comes to future partners, this is one of the most important aspects that you can possibly imagine. There are a lot of men out there who are still tied to Momma, and that's not a good thing. It's nice if he respects her and does things for her. But if there's ever a conflict between you and his mother, whose side do you think he'll choose? It's better to know that at the beginning of the relationship rather than after the wedding.

"Stay away from guys who are tied to Momma's apron strings," warns Carol, who is the voice of experience. "When Brad and I first started dating, I thought that it was really sweet, the way that he was always looking after his mother. They would talk on the phone for hours, and it was nice to see that kind of tight bond. He talked to her every day and visited at least once a week. Some of my friends tried to tell me that it seemed like he was a little too wrapped up with his mother. I thought they were just exaggerating things."

"Unfortunately, Brad and I hit a rocky patch, and his mother decided that she had to get right in the middle of it. All of a sudden, I was dealing with both him and his mother, and it was too much for me to handle. I had to end the relationship. The last I heard, he was living with his mother again -- and he wasn't involved with anyone."

It's important to see how he treats the rest of his family, too -- not just his mother. The relationship that a man has with his father and with his brothers and sisters says a lot about him. These are things you can't find out just by talking about it. You have to see him with his family to get the real picture.

Remember -- how he treats his family is probably how he's going to treat you when you're married and you become a part of his family. That's why, even if you don't get any feedback from your own family, you need to see how he relates to those who are closest to him.

There's an old saying that when you marry a man, you also marry his family. On the one hand, that sounds like it might be a little simplistic, but there have been many relationships that have been severely strained because of the family's interaction. I know that it's romantic to think only of the two of you, but neither of you is going to stop seeing your family just because you're married. When you're thinking about your future together, the fact remains that we are all attached to our families.

This even applies if he's estranged from his family.

"I was with a guy that I was totally in love with," Eleanor remembers, "and he was everything that I was looking for in a man. The only thing that bothered me was that he didn't have a close relationship with his family. I could tell that he wanted that kind of relationship, though. Yet for some reason, he and his family just refused to get together and get over whatever differences they were having."

"We got engaged, and everything was going along wonderfully. Then, out of the blue, his father contacted him and said that he wanted to make amends. At first, I thought this was going to be great for our relationship. I thought that this guy was going to be thrilled to have his family back in his life. It turned out to be a disaster. Oh, things started out great. Soon after, they started to fight -- and, I got dragged into the middle of it. I tried to keep out of it, but it was nearly impossible."

"That led to fights between me and this guy, because he thought that I was taking their side against him. No matter how much I tried to tell him that wasn't the case, he didn't want to hear it. We grew more and more apart, and one morning, I woke up and I realized that I had to end it. As much as I loved this man, I knew that having his family in our lives -- and I was sure they were going to be there for a long time -- would make our relationship impossible, and I walked away."

"The good news is that I met another man, about a year later, and he and his family get along great. All of them have healthy boundaries. I'm not sure if this is going to go anywhere further, but at least I know that it can, without outside interference ruining it."

Parents and siblings aren't the only family relationships we need to be concerned with. Don't forget that many men have children from previous marriages. More than anything, it is important that you meet the children (whether adolescent or grown) early on in the relationship. This way, it gives them a chance to see you, and it gives you a chance to see what his relationship with his children is.

Dear Kathy,

I'm in a relationship with a man who is recently divorced. He and I get along

*good except when it comes to his children.
They are VERY disrespectful towards
him. I was visiting one day and his
daughter came over with her children. I
said hello to them. His six year old
granddaughter rolled her eyes at me as if
she was disgusted to see me. They don't
know the meaning of the word respect.
His way of resolving this issue is to call
our relationship off. On the other hand, he
always wants to see me. I haven't talked
to him in a couple of days. I asked him if
the relationship was over. He said he
didn't know what he wanted to do.
Should I end it, instead of waiting around
to see if he even wants to be with me or
not?*

Diane

Dear Diane,

*You say that you get along good except
for his family. That's a really big 'except.'
Even though his daughter is an adult and
on her own, she and her children are still a
big part of his life. If you continue the
relationship, this is an issue that you will
have to deal with over and over. You and
he must be able to agree on how to handle
his family if your relationship is to survive
and flourish. After all this time, his
daughter and granddaughter are probably*

not going to change the way they act toward him. That's the way they are, and that's the way he is. After all, he put up with this behavior before you came along. You will have to decide if you can live peacefully with their behavior. That means accept them the way they are and don't complain about it. If you can not, then it's time to move on to someone who doesn't have disrespectful children and grandchildren.

Diane must understand that you can't separate the man from his family. If they're disrespectful, it's because he allows them to be that way. So to critique them is just like critiquing him. I can't begin to tell you the number of relationships that have been derailed because of children in the mixture. With so many divorces, it seems like almost everyone has his children and her children to contend with. Why do you think second and third marriages fail even more than first marriages? It's so hard to blend families and have everyone get along. That's why it's vital that you and your potential partner get things straight at the outset. You don't need to waste years on someone if you can not stand to be around his children. I don't care how much you think you love him, it's not going to work.

If there are children involved, it might be a good idea to get some counseling or get some material to read at the outset so that you can understand what it takes to be in a relationship with a man who has children from previous marriages. The same is true if you have children from a previous marriage. While the children can't make your decision for you of whom to marry, it's vital to have their input about any possible future spouse. They will have to live with him too.

"When I first started dating Carl," Vicki remembers, "he mentioned that he had a daughter, and I really didn't think too much about it. She lived with her mother in Vermont, and we were in New York. She was a teenager, and Carl talked to her a couple of times a month. His wife had full custody, and I knew that I'd see Carl's daughter during holidays and when she visited, but I didn't think that she was going to factor into the relationship very much.

"But, Carl's ex-wife got sick, and she sent his daughter to stay with him. From the moment the girl met me, she and I didn't get along. Carl tried not to take sides during any disagreements that we had, but after a while, the tension in the relationship just got to be too much. I loved Carl, but I didn't like his daughter. I couldn't see any way for us to work it out and we broke up. I learned my lesson, though. I am definitely not getting involved with a man who has a kid, that's for sure."

In Vicki's case, by the way, we can also see the importance of something that we discussed earlier -- making your list of dating requirements. By dating a man with a teenage daughter, she learned that it was something she didn't want to have to deal with. 'No children from a previous marriage' went on her list of requirements. She was then able to eliminate some of the men that she was thinking about once she found that there were children involved.

The best strategy is for you to meet his family, and for him to meet yours. Of course, this doesn't mean that you have to give your family veto power. That's entirely up to you. But, at the very least, you should listen to what they have to say. They can see things that you don't, and that input can help you make your decision further down the line.

My friend's son was dating a nice young lady. They were even talking about getting married. But every time they would have an argument, she would stomp off and not talk to him for several days. He asked me about it. Like any good coach, I did not tell him what to do. I only tried to get him to realize what was really going on. I asked him, did their disagreements ever get resolved? Of course not, because she would always walk out. After a few days he would call her up and apologize, and things would be okay again. But since they never resolved anything, they would argue about the same things over and over. I asked him, "Is this the way you want your life to be? How will you ever resolve anything if she walks out every time you disagree? And one day, when you get tired of saying I'm sorry, what will happen then?" The next time they got into an argument, he told her if she walked out not to come back. You can guess what happened. She walked out expecting to hear from him in a few days. He never apologized. She called him a few days later and tried to make up, but he realized they just weren't right for each other. They broke up shortly after.

You don't need a relationship coach to point out things like that to you. You just need people who know you and care about you. This means, naturally, that you're going to want the introductions to take place sooner, rather than later -- and definitely before there's any kind of engagement.

Keep in mind that this man is going to become a part of your family -- and you're going to be a part of his. That means that if either family is negative about the relationship, it's something that you're going to have to deal with throughout the marriage, assuming there is one. It won't automatically make the relationship impossible, it will just be something you'll have to talk about and learn to deal with.

Usually we see that someone will go out of his or her way to try to get the future in-laws to like them. That makes the whole exercise rather useless. The point is for you to see them as they are and for them to see you as you are. There's no advantage to meeting the family if you're going to pretend to be someone you really aren't. You probably won't agree on everything, but at least you should be assured that you can all get along.

Remember -- you're not just marrying a man. You're marrying a family. Make it one of the criteria to consider when you're looking for the man you want to spend the rest of your life with. Don't make the mistake of not listening to your friends and family when it comes to making this very important life decision. Get input from your family and friends before you make a commitment.

Chapter Ten

Mistake #9

Settling for Too Little

Many men and women sell themselves short when they look for a mate. We all have our own idea of what we'd like the perfect mate to be. But for so many of us, we just never seem to attain that goal. We get tired of looking or worry that we'll never find someone, so we settle for someone who is merely 'good enough.' In your quest to find the perfect partner, it's important that you avoid falling into the trap of settling for too little.

Let's say you've been invited to attend a party with one of your girl friends. You want a new outfit to wear so you'll look really good (in case there are some cute guys there). First you have to decide if you want a skirt or pants, a blouse or sweater, what color and style. Once you have in mind what you want, you start to shop. You find a skirt you like but it's not the right style, so you keep looking. You find another that's the right style, but not the color you had in mind. You go on to the next store. You shop the whole afternoon and you're getting tired. The next store you go into has one that is close to what you want. You're tired of shopping so you buy it. When you wear it to the party, are you comfortable with it? Probably not, because it's not really what you wanted. So instead of feeling good about how you look you're wishing you'd kept looking for what you really wanted. It's the same when you're shopping for a partner.

There are many different reasons why women settle for too little when shopping for a partner. Let's take a look at some of the reasons why women don't hold out for what they really want.

Many of us have an image of the person that we want. And, in a lot of cases, that person we've created in our minds is physically attractive. But when it comes to finding a partner, we somehow find ourselves thinking that we can't measure up. Of course that's total nonsense. One of the lessons I learned early in life is that the inferior person that I sometimes saw when I looked in the mirror was not the person that the world saw -- and the same probably holds true for you. We tend to exaggerate our flaws in our own mind because we look at them every day. You know every little blemish and wrinkle, every extra pound, and every bit of cellulite you think you have. But others don't notice those things, and they're just not that important to the rest of the world. You might think that you're not anything exceptional, but there are people out there who would disagree with you. There are many other aspects to consider besides our physical attributes. When you get to know someone and like them, they become more physically attractive in your mind as well.

One single friend recently told me she had started dating someone who has been her friend for several years. She never thought she'd date anyone like him because he's not that physically attractive. But the more she got to know him, the more she liked him. And suddenly, he became more attractive in her eyes. So don't think you won't find the person you're looking for just because you're not good enough.

A big reason women settle is that they fear being alone. As we've mentioned earlier, men and women are social creatures. They need others in their lives -- unless they're hermits. When we're trying to find a partner who is going to be with us for the rest of our lives, we want to find him now. We're afraid of being alone, sometimes even for a few months. Some women think they must be in a relationship all the time because they don't like sitting home by themselves. If this is you, you have to find a way to get over that fear. After all, it's going to take time to find the right person. It's not something that you can rush your way through. Rather than holding out for the right person, though, we try to stave off loneliness by grabbing tightly to the next person who comes along. We tell ourselves that having a mediocre relationship is better than not having a relationship at all. That is totally wrong thinking. As long as you're in even a mediocre relationship, you're off the dating market. You'll never find the person you really want because you've stopped looking. How will you find that perfect pair of jeans if you're not out shopping?

Dear Kathy,

I've been married for 4 years to Jim. I knew when we married that he wasn't really right for me, but I was afraid I'd never find anyone else and I didn't want to be single forever. My mother tried to talk me out of it, but I thought I knew what I was doing. Soon after the wedding we started having problems. We argue all the time and seem to disagree on everything. I've tried to make it work, but I just don't think I can stick it out any longer. I recently met a man at work, Harry. He's everything I ever wanted. He's funny, smart, good looking, and makes me feel like someone special when I'm around him. I don't know what to do. Should I leave

*Jim and start a relationship with Harry?
I'm confused.*

Kim

Dear Kim,

Your problem is a common one. You seemed to be in a hurry to get married and now you're sorry you did. Make a list of the things you like and don't like about Jim. What attracted you to him in the beginning? Try to be objective. If your list of dislikes is longer than your list of likes, you may not be able to save your marriage. If you do decide to end your marriage, don't rush right into a relationship with Harry. You need to take time to evaluate what went wrong the first time and try to avoid making the same mistake again. Next time, make sure you wait to find someone who's right for you and not rush into a relationship because you don't want to be alone.

Kim's situation shows what happens when women are afraid of being alone. They end up staying with someone who they know is not right for them just so they have someone. Then, when Mr. Right comes along, they're not available.   There's nothing wrong with being single and holding out for what you want.

Some women are softies for any man with a sad story.   They have a history of always attaching themselves to men who've had a hard life and forming relationships with them.   As a relationship coach, I've spent literally hundreds of hours coaching women who felt they had to protect a man who has had a hard life, or a man who has had an unhappy childhood, or a man who has some problems.   When I come across a woman like that, I know that I'm dealing with someone who isn't actually looking for a partner. I'm dealing with someone who wants to "rescue" someone.   They think it's their job to rescue these men and make their lives better.

These are the women who usually end up with men who are physically or verbally abusive. Time after time, I've heard women tell me about their abusive boyfriends, or their boyfriend who is addicted to drugs or alcohol.   I've listened as women told me about their boyfriends who are cold and who are emotionally empty.   They'll tell me that these men in their lives have never really had love before, and they don't know how to handle it.   It's not that they're really bad men; they just haven't learned how to accept love and show love in return.   The women feel that it's their duty in life to teach this poor soul how to love.   If they just love these men enough, they will stop being abusive or stop being so cold.   In other words, they're appointing themselves this dysfunctional man's caretaker and love giver. It's sort of like the woman who sees a stray puppy along the road and takes him home. He's wild and destructive because he's never been around people enough to trust them. So even though the puppy bites at her and her friends and destroys her house, she keeps it because the puppy was abandoned and needs her love and care.

A lot of women will settle for a man who has a whole trunk full of problems. You would think that the less work there is to do on a man, the better off we'd be. But many of us don't see it that way. On some level, we find ourselves settling for an inferior man, just so that we can feel superior to him. All of those problems of his -- well, we're just going to fix them, right? You're going to take away all of his flaws and make him into a brand-new person. If he's not perfect now, he will be by the time you're finished with him. Unfortunately it doesn't work out that way. As we mentioned earlier, you can't get into a relationship and think you are going to change someone or "fix" them. That's a task that can only be handled from within. If they don't want to do it, you're not going to be able to make them. You can't turn someone into your ideal man if he's not that way already.

Now, you might be wondering why in the world a woman wouldn't go out of her way to find a man who is competent and confident and mature and stable. After all, that's probably on the list of requirements that we're all trying to fulfill, right? A lot of women feel that their value comes from taking care of others. For some reason, they are holding onto an outdated notion that as long as they have someone to care for, someone to clean up after, someone to compensate for, then they have a purpose in life.

I call it "The Aunt Bea Syndrome."

In one episode of THE ANDY GRIFFITH SHOW, Aunt Bea left Andy and Opie alone while she went to visit her sister. She worried that her men might not be able to handle things on their own, but they assured her that they would be okay. During the time she was away, Andy and Opie lived like bachelors. They ate what they wanted, when they wanted, and they made a mess of the place. But, on the day of Aunt Bea's return, the boys felt guilty about having Aunt Bea come back to such a mess. So they went into "crisis clean mode." By the time Aunt Bea walked through the door later that day, the house was immaculate. Both Andy and Opie assumed that she'd be pleased to see the house so well taken care of in her absence.

Instead, she's crestfallen.

She thinks that Andy and Opie got along so well in her absence, that she isn't really needed. Once they figure out what's happened, Andy and Opie make a mess of the place and pretend to be helpless. Aunt Bea comes to the rescue, huffing and puffing with faux exasperation at how they can't seem to do the simplest of tasks on their own. She cleans up the mess with a smile on her face and singing under her breath.

Her boys need her, after all. There are a lot of women out there who fall into The Aunt Bea Syndrome. It's not just women who fall into this trap. There are men out there who have some of these same problems.

Jeff, a realtor from Dallas, Texas, is a prime example of this.

"I always find myself attracted to girls with problems," he explains. "For some reason, I always think I can help them out. The more messed up they are, the more I want to be with them. I know part of the reason is that I always think that I can be some kind of knight in shining armor and rescue them, but it never seems to work out that way."

At least Jeff is one of those people who understands what he's doing on an intellectual level. He knows in his head that what he's doing will not work out, but when it comes to getting into a relationship, he continues to fall into the same pattern.

There are also women out there who are suffering from a martyr complex. You probably know someone like that. They find themselves partnering with an obviously flawed mate, and that enables them to engage in the game of "poor me." They show the world what they have to put up with, and they derive a certain kind of pleasure from being miserable. They're constantly telling you about their problems with their partner. Unfortunately, these women do not understand that happiness is a choice. It would scare the average person half to death to realize the power that each of us has to have all the love and happiness and success that we want. It's a lot easier to simply lower our sights and to avoid taking responsibility for our own happiness.

Earlier, we talked about not having sex too soon in a relationship, and I told you why it was so important. One of the consequences of having sex too soon in the relationship is that we stay out of a sense of guilt. After all, we've been having sex with him, right? What's he going to think if we end the relationship? I say it doesn't matter what he thinks. What matters is that you make yourself happy by finding the right person to fulfill your requirements. Whenever you discover he's not the right one for you, it's time to move on. It doesn't matter how long you've been seeing him or whether or not you've had sex. If he doesn't meet your list of requirements and measure up, end the relationship and start looking for someone who does.

In an earlier chapter, we talked about getting your family's approval before you get into a committed relationship. If your family likes him, it might be a good sign as your relationship progresses. Having said that, though, you have absolute decision-making authority to get out of a bad relationship, no matter what your family thinks. Amanda went through a hard time when she was in a relationship with a man who was wrong for her.

"It was hard," she says, "because he just wasn't making me happy. It wasn't that he treated me wrong or that there was anything that I could put my finger on. There was just something missing from the relationship, and I couldn't figure out what it was. So, I went to my mother and my sister, and I told them that I was breaking it off with Kevin."

"Both of them freaked out on me. They told me that he was perfect, and that I was a fool if I let him go. They put so much pressure on me that I stayed in the relationship, even though I didn't want to. Then, as time went past, I stayed in the relationship because I'd already invested so much time and energy into it -- and because Kevin really needed me. Still, I was totally miserable. I kept trying to make it work because Kevin was a nice guy and because my family thought he was the best thing that was ever going to happen to me."

"Eventually, though, it just wasn't enough. I couldn't take it any longer, and I told Kevin that I just didn't think that he was the right person for me. To my surprise, he told me that he had been thinking the same thing for a long time, but he didn't want to be the one to make the move. Now, both of us have people in our lives who are better suited for us, and we're still very good friends." Don't settle for someone just because your family likes him. They don't have to live with him, you do.

One of the most common arguments for staying in a relationship in which we "settle" is that we think it will get better. We tell ourselves that the man is going to change. Sure, he's got some problems, but he's working on them, right? Things can't stay like this forever, can they? He's going to change because he loves me. If we love each other we don't need anything more. The truth is he's never going to change. With men and women, what you see is what you get.

But, let's say that he does change, eventually, but that it takes years. Is that fair to you? Should you have to give up years of your life so that the man you settled for is now someone more like the man you're looking for? You wouldn't settle for a pair of flats when you wanted high heels. Those shoes are still going to be flats 10 years from now. You shouldn't settle for a man who's not right for you. He's probably not going to change any more than those shoes will.

Let's say that you take your car to an auto shop for repair. You've got a hole in the fuel line and the brakes are shot. What would you do if the mechanic came up to you and said,

"You know, we can fix this, but it's going to take a couple of years. We'll work on it a little at a time, and sooner or later, you'll have your car the way that you want it." It sounds absurd. Yet so many women are willing to get into relationships with men who are wrong for them, and they literally spend years trying to make these men over into the man they want. They shed tears, they have fights, and they make themselves crazy over what's going on. In the end, there's not even a guarantee that the man is going to change for them. That's a terrible way to go through relationships. At least the auto shop will give you a 30 day guarantee.

There are so many people out there who could be a good match for you. You don't need to go into a relationship that needs so much work. All relationships will have their ups and downs. You shouldn't be starting out with one that's difficult from the beginning. You don't have to waste precious years of your life on trying to fit a square peg into a round hole. You may be able to make it work, if you apply enough pressure on the peg and enough force and enough sweat in the process -- but why make yourself crazy? You don't have to work that hard.

If there's one message in this book that I want you to understand, it's that we only have one physical life on this world, so we need to make the most of what time we have. Life is too short to spend time trying to make an unsuccessful relationship into one that's successful.

Studies show that it gets harder and harder to meet new people as you get older. In fact, for women over 50, there are fewer and fewer men every year compared to the number of women. The competition for finding a man is only going to keep getting tougher. That's just the reality of the situation. That's why it's so important to make smart choices when we're young and not waste time of someone who's not right for you.

You can't argue with the demographics. None of us is going to have endless tries at finding romance and happiness. I don't want you to panic and think that you're running out of time. There are always stories of couples who get together in their 60's, 70's, or even 80's. But you need to realize that the choices do get more limited the older you get. We each have a limited number of days on this earth. That's why the whole concept of serial monogamy needs to be eliminated from your dating plan.

You can go down the well-worn path of meeting a man, dating him for a few months, getting into an exclusive relationship with him, finding out that he's not the man for you, ending the relationship, and starting the process over again. That's what most people do today. Do this a few times and you'll find that 10 or 15 years have gone by, and you still don't have the lifelong relationship of love and happiness that you've so desperately been searching for. That's why women spend years of their lives in relationships that are not right for them only to find themselves alone again. That's why break-ups are so hard.

"For me, I always thought that the right man was going to come along," Amy told me. "I didn't know where he was going to come from, but I just thought that one day, he'd appear. In the meantime, though, I was dating a series of losers. One guy turned abusive on me. Another one was an alcoholic. Still another one slept with my best friend while I was on a business trip. Each time a relationship ended, I'd get involved with someone else, and I'd still be thinking that the perfect man for me was going to magically appear in my life."

"Looking back on it, I can see that I wasn't really being realistic. I was sort of a mess, and the chances of a decent man coming along and finding me desirable were pretty slim. The only men who were attracted to me were the ones that were screwed up because they saw that I was screwed up. The healthy men stayed away. But I finally got my head on straight, and I decided that if I was going to find the right man for me, I was actually going to have to figure out what I wanted in a man. Then I had to go out there and actually look for him. It took me five years, but I eventually found the perfect man for me...and there's no way that he would have found me, if I hadn't gone out there and sought him out."

I know there are people out there who are going to complain that this might make getting into a relationship take a little longer than you might be used to. That's a good thing. We live in a world where more and more people are settling for less and less. We go into a restaurant, and we settle for less than terrific service. We leave big tips anyway. We walk into a store and get waited on (or ignored) by rude salespersons. When we complain, the manager tells us, "It's hard to get good help," as if that's an explanation for sub-standard service. Cable companies laugh at us when we tell them that we want to have lower rates and better service.

Sometimes you don't have a choice. Sometimes you have to settle for less than perfect service, less than perfect products, or less than perfect food. Don't settle for less than perfect when it comes to your relationship.

Here's another way to look at what you're going to do. You are making an investment -- an investment in the rest of your life and in your happiness. Instead of just jumping head first into the pool, why not walk around a couple of times; get the lay of the land? Rather than just plunging blindly ahead, take a little extra time on the front end. Sure, it's not as much fun as jumping right in, but you're going to increase your chances of finding that wonderful relationship for the rest of your life if you take a little longer in the beginning.

I know we live in a world of immediate gratification. We want what we want and we want it right now. Yes, we want a great relationship, and we want it now. We don't want to take the time and the energy to make sure that we're on the right path. We just want to get it happening right now. We see that road of love, commitment, family, and we want to get going. But that road has many turns and potholes. You need to be sure you're going the right way before you reach the next stop. You don't want to have to turn around and start over again.

The more time you take before getting into a relationship, the less time you're going to spend trying to make that relationship work. The more people that you encounter before you get into a relationship, the more likely the chances are that you're going to find the right person that you want in your life forever. The more you are willing to eliminate bad choices before you get involved with someone, the greater the odds are that you're going to end up with a great choice as a partner.

When we buy a new house or a new car, most of us do some checking. We find out about the builder of the house, the manufacturer of the car. We examine each room. We kick the tires and look under the hood. Doesn't it make sense to do the same thing when it comes to finding our life partner?

This is the biggest decision of your life -- bigger than the right job, bigger than the right house or the right car. You're looking for the person who is going to bring happiness and joy to you for the rest of your life. Don't make the mistake of settling for someone who's not right for you; settling for too little. Take time to find the right one because you're worth it. You don't have to settle for anything less.

Chapter Eleven

Mistake #10

Not Following Kathy's One-Year Rule

I am continuously amazed at how eager and quick some women are to get themselves into a relationship and into a marriage. Keep in mind that these are the same women that have come out of bad relationships, so you would think that they'd know better. Instead, it's as if they just assumed that because the last relationship didn't work out, the next one will.

We've already discussed how most women will date a man once or twice, then consider themselves in a committed relationship. And, I would hasten to add, these are women who are bright and intelligent. It's not as if we're dealing with women here who just don't know any better.

Unfortunately too many women follow their heart. While that's not all bad, you shouldn't let the heart overrule what the head is telling you. It doesn't matter if you're a lawyer or a salesperson or a hair dresser -- when it comes to affairs of the heart, some women just don't think as clearly as they should.

So, these women date a man a couple of times, and things are going well. They're doing okay together. At that point, the woman decides that they're taking themselves off the market and that they're going to enter into an exclusive relationship. In many cases, the woman decides this on her own. The man isn't even put into the loop on this one. He's going along, dating this girl, and thinking that both of them are on the same page. The fact is, events are happening that he doesn't know anything about.

This reminds me of something that happened in our family.

When my son was young he wanted a puppy just like most young boys. I promised to take him shopping for a dog. Before we went on the trip to find our new pet, however, I talked it over with my son, telling him that adding a pet to the family was a big commitment that would last between 10 and 20 years. I told him to take his time, and to look at pets from different places -- from breeders and from pet stores and from the humane society. Want to guess what happened? The first breeder we visited had a litter of puppies. That was it for him. No more looking -- our perfect pet was somehow in that group of puppies.

Now, consider that this is precisely how some women shop for their life partners. They will go out into the dating world, and date one or two men. After a couple of dates, they make the decision that one of those two men is "The One." Sounds rather scary to me. To think that someone would make a decision such as marriage, a decision that is supposed to be for the rest of your life, based on only dating a handful of men is incredible.

Now, keep in mind that the man that she's chosen is a virtual stranger. Oh, sure, she might think she knows everything there is to know about him, but the truth is that she knows very little. And, what happens when we enter into a relationship with someone who is basically a total stranger to us? If you've been paying attention at all to any of the previous chapters you already know the answer. It's not going to last and we endure another round of heartbreak and disappointment.

"When I met Nick," film producer Julianna recalls, "I had just broken up with my fiancé of five years. Nick was an actor, but he wasn't like other actors -- there was a depth to him that I found very appealing. He was smart and clever and sensitive and thoughtful."

"We went out on a couple of dates, and during those dates, we really got to know each other. At least, I thought that I was getting to know him. We were talking for hours at a time, and I decided that I had been lucky enough to find the perfect guy for me. After just a few months, we were living together. That's when things started to go downhill."

"I found out that he wasn't the man that I thought he was at all. He had always been on his best behavior when we were out on a date. But when he was at home, he was like a totally different person. He displayed a lot of anger and it surprised me. There was an edge to him that I hadn't seen when we were first dating, and it was thanks to a good friend that I was able to get out of the relationship before something bad happened."

Consider this -- if you dated a number of men, and then married and remained married for the rest of your life, over 95 percent of your relationships failed. Only one relationship lasted forever, that's the way it should be. But that's not what usually happens. Most women have only a few relationships, and they all fail. Think about the fact that most marriages fail (counting second and third marriages, as well), and you'll see that the system of dating most people have been using just doesn't work any longer. The reality is that it never did.

Let's say that you've dated a man once or twice, and now, you're exclusive. Most couples decide to get engaged within the first 12 months. (The ones that don't can take several years -- or not at all.) Now, when does commitment start in that relationship? If you said "At the wedding ceremony," you'd be making a mistake. The truth is that commitment starts with the engagement -- or, it should. You see, the wedding is just the formalization of the commitment, and the declaration in front of witnesses.

The real commitment is when one person proposes marriage, and the other person accepts. So many women are committing to men that they've only known for a few months. They think they know him well enough to determine that they want to spend their life with him. At least, they want to spend all their dating time with him and not see anyone else.

Listen very carefully -- if you've dated and known a man less than 12 months, you don't really know him. Sure, this might sound like an arbitrary number, but I've found that it helps to have guidelines to help us decide when we're in the right relationship. I was watching a program on TV a few weeks ago about weddings. The show had 2 couples and followed them as they planned their weddings showing you what they did and how the wedding day turned out. I was shocked that both of the couples on this show had met and become engaged within 4-6 months. I don't usually watch such shows, but now they had my attention. I had to watch the next episode. Sure enough, both of those couples had met and become engaged within 6 months as well. I'd like to see a follow up on how many of them are still married after 5 years. I'll bet it's not very many. You just can't know enough about someone in that short a time to be sure if they're right for you.

That's why I've come up with a system to help you. In my system -- Kathy's "One Year" Rule -- you do not become engaged for at least one complete year from the first date. Sure, I know this flies in the face of those wonderful stories about meeting someone and knowing within two weeks that this was the person you were going to spend the rest of your life with. For every one of those cases that actually works out, I can give you one hundred that ended in tears and frustration. We're trying to be realistic here, not present some fantasy.

Why one year? Well, for starters, one year will give you enough time to get to know someone without wasting years and years. You have twelve months to explore each other's background, to find out what they really like and what they really don't like, to see who that person really is.

When you engage in the one year rule, you'll be putting yourself on a timetable, as well. You'll be telling yourself, "Okay, I've got twelve months here to find out if this is the person I really want to spend the rest of my life with." Otherwise, you could be one of those people who gets into a relationship and never takes the time to find out if you're with the right person. You might just coast along for years until the relationship finally falls apart, or until you decide to settle for what you've got.

One friend, Julie, started dating a guy while she was in college. I'll call him Steve. Julie and Steve dated all through college. Even after they both graduated and had full-time jobs, they still dated exclusively. This went on for ten years. Finally, they started talking about getting married. But Julie then discovered something she'd probably known all along. She didn't want to marry Steve. He was a nice guy, but he was not the one she wanted to spend the rest of her life with. Once she admitted that to herself, the relationship was over. Within a year, Julie had met another man, the one she's been married to now for 20 years. Things worked out okay for Julie, but look at how much time she wasted with Steve. How many men could she have met during that time that would have been better suited for her? If Julie had put more thought into her relationship with Steve she would have realized sooner he was not right for her. Poor Steve, he wasted 10 years of his life on Julie as well. I'm not saying you have to make a decision within a year, but 10 years is a bit excessive. You can surely tell in less time than that.

In that year, you can find out how he deals with your family, how you deal with his family, and even how each of you will interact with the others' friends. That should give you plenty of time to see him how others see him, and how he reacts to those people in your life who are close to you. Remember, you're not going to wait until a week before the wedding to introduce him to your family.

Lastly, during that year, you'll have gone through a 12-month period together, and you'll be with each other through each season -- spring, summer, fall, and winter. You'll have been with each other through the holidays. Holidays sometimes bring out the best, and worst, in people. You want to find this out before you make a commitment. And yes, you'll have each experienced a lot of different moods with the other person. That's good. The more you see of each other, the more you'll be able to determine if this is the right relationship for you.

Some people think that when they're trying to find out if they're with the right person, they need to always be on their best behavior. They don't want to do anything to upset their date; they sure don't want to rock the boat. Just the opposite is true. You don't want to be intentionally ugly, put you have to be yourself. You're trying to find the person that you're going to spend the rest of your life with. That means letting that person see you when you're in a bad mood is good. If you marry this man, he's going see you when you're in a bad mood. You won't be in a good mood every day of your life. Conversely, you want to see him when he's in a bad mood. You want to see how he acts when he is angry and how he handles life's disappointments.

At the beginning of our dating cycle, most of us are able to put up a good front -- at least for the first few months. We're able to keep our true selves hidden, for the most part. But by the end of the first year, it's much more likely that our true selves will come out -- and his true self will come out, too. That's what you want to see. If the attraction is still there after one year, you have a promising long-term relationship.

There's something important that you need to understand, however. You are not committed during this first year -- not even if you're dating him exclusively. At any time, during the first year, you can walk away from the arrangement if you find a requirement that isn't being met or if you find that too many of the traits that you'd like to have in a mate are missing. This is an important concept to remember this. Just because you've been dating for a year does not mean you can't walk away any time you discover he's not right for you.

When you go into your "one year" period, you need to be honest with yourself. Don't go in with the intention of sticking it out for a year, so that you can get engaged. Rather, go in with both eyes open, and tell yourself, "I have a year to find out if this person is the one that I'm going to spend the rest of my life with, and if he isn't, I'm going to walk away from it." Always remember that if either of you finds someone better has come along, you're free to break up and date that other person.

Dear Kathy,

I've been dating Joe for almost one year. We get along well and I think he's going to ask me to marry him soon. The problem is there's a new guy at work that I really like. I don't know what's come over me, but I find myself making up excuses to talk to him. He always seems glad to see me and is very flirty. What should I do? I thought I really loved Joe, but then why do I have feelings for this new guy at work?

Karen

Dear Karen,

Since you've been with Joe for almost a year, you're past that infatuation stage of the relationship. You've gotten more comfortable with him and things are now more routine. That's the way relationships go. The new guy at work is, well, new. He's exciting because you don't know much about him yet. He's mysterious and there's the fantasy of what he could be like. Sounds like you're not really sure that Joe is the one you want to spend your life with. That's okay. You can take more time. But you need to think really hard about the two of them. Is the possibility of dating the new guy worth breaking off your relationship with Joe? You can't have both. Don't make a commitment to Joe right now; you can continue your relationship as it is. In a few more months, the new guy at work will either wear off or seem more attractive to you. That will help you make your decision.

Keep in mind that during the one year that you're dating, you're probably going to meet more attractive people who could be possible partners -- and the same is true for him. How does that make you feel? When you look at him and compare him to others out there, does he still seem to be the one -- or would you rather have the freedom to leave and pursue other relationships? Just as in Karen's situation above, there may come a time when you will have to choose to stay in your current relationship or take a chance on a new one. There's nothing wrong with pursuing a new one, if that's what you want. Only you can decide what's right for you. Yes, you want input from your family and friends, but it is ultimately your decision. Just remember, you should stay with a relationship because that's what you want, not because that's what you need. Don't stay with someone just because you need to have a man in your life.

When you finally do make a commitment, everything changes. You no longer are looking to see if the new guy at work might be available. True commitment means you're out of the dating market — forever. It's the nature of commitment. That's what it's all about. Commitment is a very powerful addition to a relationship. It means that you know even though there will be problems in your relationship in the future, you will work them out together. Every relationship has problems, and if we're being honest with ourselves (which is the whole purpose of what we're doing), we accept that there will be problems down the road. We might not know what those problems are, but we know that, because we are in a committed relationship we are going to work them out. The problems will be dealt with and resolved together, not by walking out the door.

This is because both you and your partner are committed to the relationship -- as well as to each other. Most women want security in their lives. There's nothing more secure than knowing that your partner is committed to keeping your relationship together not matter what happens ahead. It's a wonderful feeling to be that secure in your partner and in your relationship.

"Before I met William," Donna remembers, "I always had a sort of dread in the relationships I was in. Whenever a problem came up, I always felt like I had to handle it alone. I didn't want to put any stress on the relationships because I was afraid my boyfriends would leave if things got tough. It was both exhausting and depressing. I was always trying to deal with things because I didn't want any of my boyfriends to have to worry. It just seemed to always a part of my relationships."

"But, when William came along, something happened. He was the first man who really treated me with respect. He treated me like I was someone worthwhile, and even though it took me a while to understand what he was doing, I eventually came around. Once I realized how supportive William was, it was evident what had been missing in my past relationships. But, the best thing about him was that he was really there for me. He wanted the relationship to work as much as I did, and that meant that he was right by my side when I had to deal with things. That was the greatest feeling in the world. Knowing that he was there, knowing that he wasn't going to leave me, knowing that the two of us had something that was worthwhile and beautiful -- it was wonderful."

There's something else that you should know about commitment. I just told you that when you commit to someone you take yourself out of the dating market, permanently. Here's the bad news. Even when you are in a committed relationship, someone better WILL come along. At some point in your life you will probably meet someone who would have been perfect for you. Your partner probably will too. You're not looking for someone else, but they're still out there.

Now, before you get all bent out of shape, think about that for a moment. You can not know for sure if your partner is the absolute best person for you because the only way to know that is to date every eligible and available man out there. Unless you compare them all, you have no way of knowing if you've ended up with the very best. That's because there are many men out there who will be a good match for you. If you follow the advice in this book, you'll end up with one of them. But there are still a lot out there. Someday you'll meet one of them.

Almost anyone who's been married for a few years knows this to be true. You'll meet someone who seems just perfect for you. You're tempted and you want to get to know them better. This is how affairs get started. But when you're in a committed relationship you will turn away. Commitment means that even if you meet someone who you are attracted to, you will not act on it. In fact, you will do what you need to do to make sure nothing happens with that person.

Odds are there's another person for you out there, somewhere. Yes, even though you haven't met that person, there are other people on the face of this planet who are so perfect for you that the two of you would mesh totally and completely. It doesn't matter, though. You're looking for someone to spend the rest of your life with, and I'm telling you that you are going to be able to find that someone, but he won't be the only one. If there was truly only one person out there who was perfect for you, that would be really depressing. You odds of ever finding him would be greater than winning the lottery. So be glad that there are many men out there who will be good matches for you. Just be aware that one day you will meet another one.

So, what makes a relationship really succeed, then? It's all about the commitment. You see, once you're committed, you've declared that this man is the one for you. You've said to the world, "Hey, I've been around, I've seen what's out there, and this is the man that I want to spend the rest of my life with." You take yourself off the market and because you've made a commitment, you stay off the market. Even if, and when, someone better comes along, you're not available. You're with this person, and this is the one that you've chosen.

Want to know a wonderful secret? The longer you're married, the more perfect your partner is going to become. That's right -- the more years that you've put in with your husband, the bigger advantage he's going to have over any other man who might be a good match for you.

You see, he can give you something that no one else can. He can give you a history.

"When I first got married," Mary remembers, "my mother told me that the longer George and I were married, the more handsome and the more perfect he was going to be. I didn't understand what she was talking about until our tenth wedding anniversary. We were sitting in a restaurant, just the two of us, it suddenly hit me. I thought about everything that we'd been through together -- the birth of our first child, the loss of his father, our first house. I had so many memories and George was a part of all of them, and I suddenly knew just what my mother was talking about. In that one moment, when I was looking at him, I felt such incredible love and joy at having him as my husband that I started crying. Poor George thought that something was wrong, and his concern made me cry even harder." Don't ever underestimate the power of a shared history.

When you've got a past together, when you've built up a tower of memories, you've got an emotional bank account, and those memories are your balance. The next time you see someone who seems to be better for you than your husband, just think about all the events and emotions that you've shared with your husband. You've seen each other at your best, and you've seen each other at your worst. More than likely, you've been together in sickness and in health, and for better and for worse. A good part of your life is with your husband, and the memories that you've built up together will never be shared by anyone else.

In essence, you've built up a life together, and that gives your man the advantage over anyone else that comes along. Yeah, the other guy might be more handsome and might have more money and might be more successful -- but he hasn't been there, the way that your husband has.

Are you beginning to see why the "one year" rule is so important? What it does is free you from viewing your potential partner through the eyes of an infatuated lover. By spending 12 months together, by making sure that both of you are seeing the true nature of the other, you're going to be able to more realistically determine if this is the man that you want to spend the rest of your life with. And once you've made a commitment, you will be assured that you've made the right decision. No second guessing because you spent the time you needed to know for sure.

All of us are looking for the best relationship possible, and that's why it's something that shouldn't be rushed into. It might seem like taking a year to find out if you're with the right person is a long time. But there's no substitute for putting in the time it takes to really get to know someone. The truth is, if you think about everything that it entails, it's a good time investment. After all, wouldn't you rather take the time to find out if the home you want to move into is worth the investment, rather than just rushing in, signing a contract, and then discovering that the beams are rotting and the wood is termite-infested?

Don't you think that you should take as much care in the right relationship? Think of it this way -- by holding off for one year, by taking the time to really get to know the other person and by letting them get to know you, you are investing your time into something that might well turn out to be the best thing that ever happened to you. You don't want to blow it by rushing into things too soon. You don't want to make the same mistake many women make of rushing into a committed relationship before they know for sure it's right for them. A little time taken now can save a lot of heartache in the future.

Chapter Twelve

Mistake # 11

Marrying for All the Wrong Reasons

In today's modern world, you may think it's old fashioned to get married. You can legally share everything you have with someone else without a ceremony. So why would a couple get married?

Well, the official reason is because they are in love and want to spend the rest of their lives together. If we look at both tradition and religion, we're taught that two individuals come together and become one. From that union, a new entity is born -- a married man and woman, whom no one shall break apart. This concept is both romantic and spiritual.

Let's face it, though -- is this what really happens? Take a good look around you, and you'll see other things happening all the time.

Many of us have attended a wedding where it was obvious to the guests that the couple was definitely not in love. There's often a collective wisdom that seems to know what's really going on, even if the bride or groom are in denial. It might even have happened in your own life already.

Some of you out there are going to object that this is all nonsense; that love and commitment are the only reasons people should marry. You're absolutely right. Love and commitment ARE the only reasons that couples should get married.

That's the ideal, naturally. However, the reality is completely different. Many people marry for very different reasons. It's those couples who have more problems with the marriage. In fact, I've observed that the couples who marry for reasons other than love and commitment are the ones most likely to divorce. The reason for this is simple -- the circumstances surrounding the other reasons will change throughout life, and that will nullify the reasons to stay married. In addition, when a couple has married for all the wrong reasons, eventually one or both partners will decide that life is too short to tolerate a marriage in which love and commitment are not the top priority.

Now, you might be reading this and wondering, "I don't get it. If love and commitment are what marriage is all about, why would anyone marry for any other reason?" Good question. If you think about it, though, you probably know someone who has done exactly that. If you've been married before, take a long hard look at your previous marriage. Did either you or your ex marry for some reason other than love and commitment? So let's take a look at some of the other reasons. Some of these are examples that you might recognize in other couples. Some of them might be reasons that you've used yourself.

Most women dread being alone. They have heard stories about the old spinster who lives miserably by herself and is never able to find a partner. They don't want this for themselves. Then, they find themselves in a relationship with a man who isn't around all that much. But rather than look for someone better for them, they stay in this relationship because they want to get married. They don't want to be alone. It's as if the marriage will somehow turn their boyfriend from someone who is neglectful into an attentive husband. How ironic it is that women will marry someone who is emotionally distant because they don't want to grow old alone. You and I both know that this isn't quite how things work out, however. They end up exactly where they didn't want to be; alone.

Many women are pressured by their family, especially their parents, to marry. As women get older, for some it's even as young as being in their thirties, they often find themselves subjected to that same old tiring question delivered by family members, "So, when are you going to get married?" In some cases, there's the time-honored rude analogue, "When are you going to get a man?" It's as if there's some kind of blight on the family to have a single adult woman around. Maybe all the other women are afraid she will try to steal their husbands away. Or maybe all the men are afraid their wives will see how much the single woman is enjoying her life and they'll want to be single again, too. Either way, there's nothing wrong with being single until you're ready to get married. Whether you haven't found the right person yet or you just enjoy being single, don't let family members pressure you into a marriage you don't want.

I call this one "having a license to make a baby." Some women get married because they want to have children. I'll be the first to admit that most of us don't give this one much thought any longer. Gone are the days when a woman was marked for life with a big scarlet A if she had a child before she got married. After all, approximately half of all babies born in the United States are born to parents who are not married (or are not married to each other). When you look at it, having a baby with your spouse can almost be a bit quaint and old-fashioned.

Marriage is a bond between a man and a woman. I'll be the first one to admit that having children within the marriage can be an added joy. I have children of my own. But let me tell you a hard truth, children are not a necessary part for a good marriage. They are optional. These days, not everyone wants to have children. Women can no longer assume that the man they marry will want to have children. Men can no longer assume that every woman wants to have children. This means that the decision to have them needs to be mutual and it's something that needs to be discussed before you make a commitment.

Otherwise, you might find yourself getting married just so that you can legitimize having children, and what does that say about your commitment to your man? What, then, is the man's role in your life? It puts him in the Number Two position, and all but relegates him to the role of sperm donor. It shouldn't be that way.

Your spouse should always come first in your life. I can practically hear the gasps out there. You're reading this and you're thinking, "Wow. For a relationship coach, you really don't know what you're talking about."

In fact, I'm well aware of what I'm saying. Just because many of you may not agree doesn't negate the truth of the situation. You see, I believe the marriage vows. That means your spouse is Number One in your life, and should come before your parents and before your children.

Now, I'm not saying that you shouldn't love and care for your children. That would be totally absurd. What I'm saying is that when you have a stable marriage of love and commitment, that's the foundation of your marriage. That is the firm bedrock upon which all else is built. When you put your spouse first, it means that you recognize the natural order of life. When you're young, you live with your family, and you are taken care of. Then, you grow up, and you leave the home of your parents so that you can become your own person. You become an adult.

Then, as an adult, you find yourself in various relationships, and you experience more of life and what it means to grow as a person. Eventually, the adult that you've become will freely enter into marriage with another human being and you'll become part of an inseparable couple, bound together by love and by a deep commitment to one another and to the marriage itself.

You may or may not have children. Eventually, your parents will pass on, and if you have children, they will grow up and leave, becoming independent adults just as you did. Only the marriage endures. This is the circle of life.

Friends, acquaintances, parents, and even children come and go. Your marriage is the one permanent relationship you have throughout your entire adult life. It is the single primary relationship that you'll have for the rest of your life. At least, that's the way it should be.

If a woman tells me that her children come first in her life, I can immediately see why her marriage is in trouble. The first problem is that the husband has just been relegated to the Number Two position in the family, and this causes friction in the marriage dynamic. He didn't get married just so his wife could be a mother. He got married because he wanted a partner, but now he's been replaced by the children in a sense. His wife may still love him, but most of her time and energy is spent caring for the children, not with him.

Dear Kathy,

I need help with my marriage. I've been married for 8 years to Sarah. We now have 2 children who are 6 and 4. The problem is that Sarah spends so much time with the kids that there's never any time for me. I know that sounds selfish, but we never get to spend time alone. Every night she's taking one of the kids to dance, soccer, or piano lessons. We rarely all sit down and eat together. By the time she gets home and gets the kids to bed, she's exhausted. I'm lucky if we get ten minutes together before she falls asleep. I love my children dearly, but I miss my wife. What should I do?

Tim

Dear Tim,

I have bad news for you — it's probably going to get worse. As your children get older and involved in more activities, you'll probably have less time with your wife. You and Sarah need to fix this problem now before it becomes too great to overcome. You are not being selfish to want time alone with your wife. That's why you got married. You and Sarah need to have a frank discussion about this issue and come to some agreement.

First, I recommend all couples have a 'date night' once a week. This is just you and her, away from the kids. Get a babysitter and get out of the house. It doesn't have to be expensive. My husband and I used to go to the local fast food joint and just sit and talk sometimes. But it has to be just you two; cell phones and pagers are not allowed.

Secondly, you need to talk about how many activities the kids are involved in. Can you cut some of those out, can you accompany your wife to some so you two can be together, can you take over some of the duties so your wife gets a chance to rest? These are all questions you will have to answer. It's always difficult for couples to balance their role as parents and spouses. Your wife should understand that she doesn't have to devote every minute to her children in order to be a good mother. I often find that the children are very happy to just stay home and play, and not have so many activities. Think about what you can do to help the situation, and then have a talk with your wife. I'm sure the two of you can agree on something. After all, you're married to each other, not your children.

Tim's situation shows what can happen when a woman devotes all her time to her kids. Don't get me wrong. Children require a lot of care. Especially when they are infants and toddlers, you have to devote a lot of time caring for them. There's just no way around that. But I'm talking about the women who didn't really want a husband to share their life with; they just wanted someone to be the father of their children. Since their main reason for getting married was to have children, they don't pay much attention to their spouse once they have the children they wanted.

The second problem is that many of these women have a martyr complex. What this means is that they have this compulsion to subordinate their needs for the sake of the children. At the same time, they also feel the need to subordinate their husband's needs for the sake of the children. These women live and breathe for their children. They enroll their children in so many different sports and activities that every night is spent at some practice or rehearsal. She only sees her husband when it's time to turn out the light at night. I'm sure that you know someone like that. You might even be someone like that. They are involved in the lives of their children to an incredible degree -- doing things that are above and beyond what other parents might be doing.

Something happens, though. The children grow up and they leave home. Now, twenty years have gone by, and the women discover that they have no lives of their own. How can they? They've just spent nearly a quarter of a century living the lives of their children. There's something else they might discover they don't have. Their husband.

You see, the husband has gotten tired of waiting around for his wife. He married so he could have a wife, not just someone to care for the children. He could hire someone for that. But he can't hire someone to share his life with; someone to support him and comfort him when he's down; someone to share his joy when he's up. Sure, the needs of the children are being met, but his are being ignored. So, in many cases, the man will find someone who is willing to put him into the Number One position again. Not because he no longer loves his wife, but because he wanted a marriage of love and devotion.

There are other, more selfless men, who will stay in an empty marriage for the sake of the children. We see this all the time. But, what happens when the children grow up and move away? In many cases, when the children are gone, so is the husband.

This is one of the reasons that you see so many marriages break up when the couple is in their late forties and early fifties. Sometimes, the couple will say that they "grew apart." That's not the case. The truth is,they were never "together" as a couple. Instead, they just spent twenty years hitched to the same wagon. Unfortunately, once the wagon is empty (meaning, the children are gone), they find there's no reason to stay together and they wind up going their separate ways.

In a marriage like this, nothing really went bad. Rather, the marriage started off poorly, and it came about for all the wrong reasons. Had the couple made each other the centerpiece of the marriage, the second half of their lives (and their marriage) would have been a success. There's an old saying and it's one that's well worth repeating: "The best thing a man can do for his children is to love their mother." I absolutely believe that. If you practice this and if your spouse practices this, both your marriage and your children will absolutely be fine.

Another reason some women marry is because they feel they have few choices. And as they get older, the choices are fewer. This is nonsense. While your choices do get fewer as you get older, you still have plenty left. If you've read this far, you should realize that you always have options. If you've been following what I teach in these pages, you'll see that you have a lot of choices. I know that some of you are going to disagree with me, but just hear me out.

I've done some research and I've discovered that in an average-sized city, the typical woman has about 400 men within five years of her age, and who fall into the category of "potential partners." Sure, they're not all going to be well-adjusted, clean, polite, loving people. We've already covered the fact that there are a lot of losers out there. You only need one good man, though.

So, as you can see, your challenge isn't that there are no available men. Instead, your challenge is going to be to meet them all. You'll want to screen them, you'll want to sort them, and you'll want to compare them to your list of requirements. That's what this book is all about. But don't be deceived into thinking that there aren't many men out there for you to choose from. The problem really is that there are too many. You need to know how to choose the right one.

"It's funny," Lori recalls, "but when I was single, I went through a series of bad relationships. I kept thinking that there were no good men out there. At least, I hadn't met any. I was actually heading for a marriage with someone who was the wrong one for me. I didn't love the guy, but he was pretty good to me, and I told myself that I was getting older, and that meant that I was going to have fewer and fewer choices."

"Of all people, my eighty-year-old grandmother was the one who opened my eyes. She told me that the worst thing that any woman could do was to get married because she didn't think there was anyone better out there. She and my grandfather had been married for over fifty years, and she told me that the secret to their success was that she had held out for the right man. Even when all of her younger friends were getting married, she didn't worry. 'I knew that when I married, it was going to be forever, so I wanted to make sure that I picked the right man.'

"When she told me that, it was like a light bulb went off. All of a sudden, the panic that I'd been having that I wasn't going to find the right man went away, and I was able to start thinking rationally. The moment I did that, I realized that I had been about to make a serious mistake, and I called the engagement off. It was tough but my family and friends stood by me. Six months later, I met the man that I was going to spend the rest of my life with. If I hadn't held out, I know that I'd be in a miserable marriage, right now."

Believe it or not, we're still living in an age where women are getting married just so they can have the fairy tale wedding. I've seen it before, and I'm sure that you have, too. You meet the bride, and she's so obsessed with the fancy wedding that all she can talk about is the wedding dress and the church and the cake and the flowers and the wedding itself. The groom almost seems like an afterthought. That's because he is. He's there more as a prop than as a partner. The woman is so wrapped up in being the star of the show that she barely notices the groom is there.

These are women who are thinking, "This is what I've waited for my entire life. My mother had a big wedding. My sister had a big wedding. Now, it's finally time for my big wedding." These women will usually find some poor sap to go along with their wedding plans. The wedding day comes, and the wedding is absolutely gorgeous -- it's like a dream come true.

When the wedding is over and it's just the couple, these women find out it's not like they thought it would be. I guess because they had a fairy tale wedding they think the marriage will magically be wonderful too. But when reality sets in and there's a marriage and a husband to deal with, and it's all downhill from there. That's not really surprising because they didn't really want the marriage, they wanted the wedding.

If there's one thing that you should have learned by now, it's that you can find a man and you can find love at any age. There is no "right time" to get married. If you're a happy, successful, single woman, that's fine. Rejoice! Enjoy yourself and enjoy your single life.

Marriage should be a conscious, deliberate choice -- a choice made because you've found someone to share the rest of your life with. That way, when you meet the right man and make the decision, you'll get married for all the right reasons. You won't be getting married because being single was miserable or because your lifeclock was winding down. Instead, you'll be getting married because being a couple will be even better than your wonderful single life.

Many women get married because they want security. Not the security of a steady loving relationship, but financial security. They think that a husband will provide for them so they won't have to worry about trying to live on just their salary, or maybe they won't have to work at all. If that's why you want to get married, you're in for a rude awakening. There is no such thing as a marriage for financial security. You might marry someone who has a lot of money and you might think that you're now set for life, but the fact is that the man you've married could divorce you down the road and find someone younger, someone prettier, or someone skinnier. And if you do get divorced, don't assume that you're going to get a nice settlement out of it. If you married someone wealthy, the odds are that he didn't get there by being foolish with his money. He's going to hire the best attorneys that his money can buy, and his attorneys are going to be better than the attorneys that you can afford. So you might not be as financially secure as you thought.

If any of this has even entered your mind, you need to step back and take a long, hard look at where this might head. After all, you're not even married yet, and you're already wondering about how you'll fare in a divorce. We're also living in a day and age of something called the "prenuptial agreement." This means that before a rich man will consent to marriage, his attorneys make the future bride sign a document that says if the marriage doesn't last; each party will leave with what they came with -- plus whatever other concessions might have been added.

Remember there are no guarantees in life. You may fall in love with a wealthy man and marry him only to have him lose his job and his fortune tomorrow. If you and your spouse are typical Americans with typical incomes, there's no guarantee you will have those same jobs, or any job, next year. Life is just not that certain. Over the past few years, many people have lost their jobs – jobs they thought they'd have for their entire life.

So, the bottom line is that if you're getting married because you want financial security, you might want to rethink things. Your wedding vows will say "for richer or poorer". If you marry someone only for the "richer", that marriage is in trouble from the start. Plus, if you do decide to go ahead and marry for money, part of the bargain is going to be having sex, and that means that if you're having sex for money -- well, there's a term for that kind of woman.

Some women are rescuers. These women have a unique kind of vision. They look at a man, and they don't actually see the man. Instead, they see the man the way he can be, after he's "fixed." These are the women who see such "potential" in a man, and make a conscious decision that they're going to help that man achieve whatever he needs to achieve.

They look at a man, and they see a defective, broken person who needs to be fixed, or saved, or rehabilitated. Yes, he's a pathological liar. Yes, he drinks too much. Yes, he's got a gambling problem. No matter. These women are going to save these men. They're going to get married, and they are going to help that man stop lying or stop drinking or stop gambling. Naturally these poor women wake up one day and discover that the joke's been on them, because no one can rescue anyone else.

If you see someone drowning and you jump in to save them, you'd better be prepared to knock that person out. In many instances, the drowning person will inadvertently pull you under. They'll take you down with them in an effort to keep themselves afloat. In the same way, if you see someone who has a serious problem, you need to understand that getting involved with that person is going to put you in the line of fire with that problem, as well. They will pull you down with them in their effort to keep gambling, or keep drinking, or keep lying

All of us have to conquer our own demons and overcome our own fears. No one can do that for us. So, if you get married and decide to devote the rest of your life trying to fix someone, you will have a very difficult road. In the end, you're going to realize that you've just wasted your life. Plus, you need to consider the object of all your effort. Do you really think that he's going to appreciate all that you're doing for him? Since he's not the one who wants to change, you can bet he won't. If you want appreciation, buy a dog. They appreciate you even when you're mad at them.

As we've seen here, there are a lot of reasons people get married. Many of them are not good reasons and only lead to more heartache and eventual divorce. Don't marry for the wrong reason and think you can fix it later on. Marry for the wrong reason and you'll wind up getting hurt and wasting years of your life.

There should be only one reason why you do get married. You get married because you love someone enough to commit to them and to the marriage, placing them above everyone else, cherishing them and knowing that you are cherished, as well. Marry for the right reason and you will have a wonderful relationship that will last the rest of your life.

Coach Kathys Dating Success System

1. **Make a list before you shop.**
   If you don't know what you want in advance, you'll settle for anything.
2. **Let the world know what you want.**
   Your perfect partner can't find you if you don't let everyone know you're available.
3. **Shop and compare.**
   If you're dating one person at a time, how do you compare?
4. **Sex can wait.**
   Love and sex are not the same. Find love first.
5. **Don't assume that he is exclusive.**
   Have the talk. Don't devote yourself to a man who is dating other women.
6. **Families matter.**
   Meet each other's family. Listen to their feedback. Like it or not, you marry the family.
7. **Follow my one-year rule.**
   No commitment until you've known him at least 12 full months. It just takes time to discover his great and not-so-great qualities.
8. **Commitment requires two things: a ring and a date.**
   Don't kid yourself: you're committed only when you both announce to the world your intentions to marry.
9. **Stop living in fantasy land.**
   Stop wishing your relationships were something they are not. Only when you are honest about your situation can you improve it.

My plan will help you find and enjoy that life-long relationship of love, respect, and commitment that you really want. This is how other women have gotten it. This is how you get it.

This is what works.

For more on these and other relationship topics visit my website at www.dearkathy.com.

About the Author

Kathy Stafford has been sought for her relationship advice by friends and family for over twenty years. Following two careers-one in healthcare and another in real estate-she decided to make the change to full-time relationship coach and author. Kathy has written more than 50 articles on relationships for single men and women and for married couples.

Her website, www.dearkathy.com, is her home base where she writes her blog, posts articles, schedules live seminars, and answers relationship questions from her base of clients and followers.

Kathy is the mother of four boys and has been married to their father, Alan, for 30 years. Off hours, her passion is tennis. She plays regularly and has been a top-ranked player in her state.

Contact Kathy at kathy@dearkathy.com

ORDER FORM FOR THIS BOOK
Relationship Remorse

To order by:
    Telephone: 866-200-3888
    Fax: 704-788-6694
    Email: orders@eplanetpublishing.com
    Internet: www.eplanetpublishing.com
    Mail: ePlanet Publishing, Inc.
                   109025 David Taylor Drive
                   Suite 100
                   Charlotte, NC 28262

Name _____

Address _____

City _____ State _____ Zip _____

Phone _____

Email _____

Please send me ____ copies of Relationship Remorse at
$19.95 Plus $4.95 Shipping and Handling in the U.S.

        Total $_____

☐Check ☐Money Order ☐Visa ☐MasterCard ☐AMEX

Card Number _____

Name on Card _____

Exp _____ Security Code _____

Prices subject to change without notice.
Call or email us for quantity pricing.